2011 RHYSLING ANTHOLOGY

Also available from the
Science Fiction Poetry Association

The Alchemy of Stars:
Rhysling Award Winners Showcase

The Science Fiction Poetry Handbook:
by Suzette Haden Elgin

The 2010 Rhysling Anthology:
The Best Science Fiction, Fantasy, and Horror Poetry of 2009

The 2009 Rhysling Anthology:
The Best Science Fiction, Fantasy, and Horror Poetry of 2008

The 2008 Rhysling Anthology:
The Best Science Fiction, Fantasy, and Horror Poetry of 2007

The 2007 Rhysling Anthology:
The Best Science Fiction, Fantasy, and Horror Poetry of 2006

2011
RHYSLING ANTHOLOGY

*The Best Science Fiction,
Fantasy, & Horror
Poetry of 2010*

EDITED BY
David Lunde

SCIENCE FICTION
POETRY ASSOCIATION

2011 Rhysling Anthology

Editor and Rhysling Chair: David Lunde
Layout and design: Robert Frazier
Cover design: Mike Allen
Printer: Lightning Source
Publisher: Science Fiction Poetry Association
Published in cooperation with: Raven Electrick Ink

Copyright © 2011
by the Science Fiction Poetry Association
in the names of the individual contributors.
All works used by permission.

ISBN: 978-0-9819643-4-8

All subsidiary rights to individual works herein belong to the author or current copyright holder. All rights pertaining to this publication itself are reserved. No part of this body of text, as presented, may be reproduced by any process in present, past, or future use without written permission of the Science Fiction Poetry Association (via its current head officer at the time of request) and pertinent copyright holders, except in the case of brief quotations embodied in critical or analytical reviews or articles. For information, write to:

Deborah P Kolodji
SFPA President

For more information on the
Science Fiction Poetry Association
visit: **www.sfpoetry.com**

CONTENTS

8   **Preface:** David Lunde

10 **The Rhysling Awards:** A Brief Introduction

10 **Acknowledgments**

12 **2011 Voting Procedures**

SHORT POEMS FIRST PUBLISHED IN 2010

13 Greg Beatty, "On Keeping Pluto a Planet"
13 F. J. Bergmann, "Chronomancy"
14 F. J. Bergmann, "Cultural Climate"
14 Bruce Boston, "Lizards and Wind"
15 Rachel Manija Brown, "Minotaur Noir"
16 Shelly Bryant, "Compelling Outward Flight"
16 Rosalind Casey, "Patience"
17 G. O. Clark, "Putting Off the Past"
18 C.S.E. Cooney, "Dogstar Men"
19 Jennifer Crow, "Hoarding Light"
19 Jennifer Crow, "We Took Our Gods"
20 Jennifer Crow, "An Incomplete Map of Death"
20 Amal El-Mohtar, "Peach-Creamed Honey"
21 Kendall Evans, "Here We Are/Implied in the Shadows/ Cast Upon Saturn's Atmosphere
22 Angel Favazza, "Call of the Wired"
23 Michael Fosburg, "My Own Ending"
24 Melissa Frederick, "Volcanoes on Io"
25 Joshua Gage, "The Shoemaker's Daughters"
25 Lyn C. A. Gardner, "Midnight Posture"
26 Jaimee Hills, "Tonight the Character of Death Will Be Played by Brad Pitt"
26 Janis Ian, "Welcome Home (The Nebulas Song)"
28 David C. Kopaska-Merkel, "A few stops on the journey"
28 Geoffrey A. Landis, "Rondel for Apollo 11"
29 B. J. Lee, "The Legend of the Flying Dutchman"
30 Rose Lemberg, "Twin-born"
31 Sarah Lindsay, "Planet Anhedonia"
32 C. S. MacCath, "A Path Without Bones"
33 W. S. Merwin, "The Chain to Her Leg"
34 Shweta Narayan, "Cave-smell"

35 Ruth Naylor, "What Mighty Force?"
36 Adrienne J. Odasso, "The Ghosts of Moody Street"
36 Stephanie Parent, "Tinkerbell"
37 Juan Manuel Perez, "Human Fighting Is Illegal"
38 Juan Manuel Perez, "El Codex Chupacabra"
38 Kelly Rose Pflug-Back, "My Bones' Cracked Abacus"
39 Karen A. Romanko, "Binary Creation Myth"
40 R. Paul Sardanas, "The Black Lotus"
41 Ann K. Schwader, "The Witch in Your Mirror"
42 Ann K. Schwader, "Scrapyard Outpost"
43 Ann K. Schwader, "Quiet In Her Mind"
44 Ann K. Schwader, "Of Ithaca & Ice"
45 Ann K. Schwader, "The Darkness Whispers (Flagstaff, AZ, 1930)"
46 Marge Simon, "Sightings"
46 Robin Spriggs, "Red Magic"
47 Sonya Taafe, "In the Earth in Those Days"
48 Sonya Taafe, "Anakatabasis"
48 Sonya Taafe, "By the Dog"
49 Sonya Taafe, "Domovoi, I Came Back!"
49 Nancy Ellis Taylor, "Genetic Memory Comes to Me"
50 Richard L. Tierney, "Yuletide"
51 Brian Trent, "A Holiday in Necropolis"
52 Patrice M. Wilson, "Images in the Dark"
53 Stephen M. Wilson, "Imagined World"
54 Stephen M. Wilson, "I, Cannibal …"
54 Stephen M. Wilson, "The Conjuror"
55 Jane Yolen, "The Gospel of the Rope"

Long Poems First Published in 2010

57 Mary Alexandra Agner, "Tertiary"
59 Tara Barnett, "Star Reservation"
60 F. J. Bergmann, "Occidental"
62 Robert Borski, "The Pantheon"
63 Robert Borski, "Bubba"
65 Bruce Boston, "Dark Rains Here and There"
67 Lisa Bradley, "The Haunted Girl"
70 C. S. E. Cooney, "Ere One Can Say It Lightens"
72 C. S. E. Cooney, "The Sea King's Second Bride"
76 Oscar L. Crawford, "My Wings Are Still Forming"
77 Malcolm Deeley, "On the Platform"
79 James S. Dorr, "Eight Top Vampire Hobbies"
81 Amal El-Mohtar and Jessica P. Wick, "Courting Song for Selkies"

- 83 Amal El-Mohtar, "The Winter Tree"
- 85 Hugh Fox and Eric Greinke, "Beyond Our Control"
- 88 Robert Frazier, "Wreck-Diving the Starship"
- 91 Joshua Gage, "Rats"
- 92 Lyn C. A. Gardner, "Homecoming"
- 94 Theodora Goss, "Ravens"
- 95 Samantha Henderson, "The Gabriel Hound"
- 97 irving, "Until the Light Fades"
- 99 Deborah P Kolodji and W. Gregory Stewart, "String Stories"
- 101 Rich Magahiz, "13 Ways of Looking at a Balrog"
- 103 Elizabeth McClellan, "Anything So Utterly Destroyed"
- 105 Jaime Lee Moyer, "A poem for no one at all"
- 106 Jaime Lee Moyer, "Rain Face"
- 108 Kurt Newton, "The Cemetery"
- 110 Steven L. Peck, "The Five Known Sutras of Mechanical Man"
- 114 W. C. Roberts, "Stargazers"
- 116 Charles Saplak, "Dragonskull: Vision of Result"
- 119 Robin Spriggs, "Blatta Infernalis"
- 119 W. Gregory Stewart and David Kopaska-Merkel, "Seasons of the Worm"
- 121 J. E. Stanley, "crossroads"
- 123 Richard L. Tierney, "Autumn Chill"
- 125 Catherynne M. Valente, "Red Engines"
- 127 Steve Vernon, "Barren: A Chronicle in Futility"
- 131 Phoebe Wilcox, "A More Significant Sun"

- 134 **The Rhysling Award Winners 1978-2011**

- 136 **SFPA Grand Master Award Winners**

- 137 **How to Join the SFPA**

A Reminiscence from the Rhysling Chair

"Why are your poems so strange?"

That was the first question the interviewer asked after I read my poem "Les Papillons". I was a bit dumbfounded—it hadn't occurred to me that my poems were strange. They were just my poems. This one was about a girl being assaulted and driven mad by butterflies. Seemed normal to me. Just about anything is strange if you look at it the right way.

It was 1969. I was being interviewed for the SUNY-Brockport Writers Forum series of videotaped interviews with contemporary authors. I'd never been interviewed by anyone for anything before. I was not famous and being interviewed about my work was pretty strange in itself, but it was encouraging. I decided I liked my work being somehow different.

Then in 1981 Gene Van Troyer told me about the SFPA and suggested I join, which I did, becoming the 115th member. Suddenly I had a family—a weird and interesting one.

I'm very grateful to the SFPA for inviting me to be this year's Rhysling Chair, not just because of the honor, but for the opportunity to read so many stunningly fine poems and reacquaint myself with the field. For the last ten years I've devoted most of my time and creative energy to translating classical and contemporary Chinese poetry in collaboration with various scholars. It was challenging and rewarding work, and I learned a lot, but it left me little time to work on my own poetry.

Reading the superb poems nominated for the Rhysling has plunged me back into the milieu in which I feel most comfortable, and I thank you all for that.

One last warning: you are going to have a very hard time deciding which of these extraordinary poems most deserves the award.

David Lunde
Chair, 2011 Rhysling Awards
May 2011

THE RHYSLING AWARDS
A Brief Introduction Adopted from Star*Line *12.5-6, 1989*

IN JANUARY 1978, Suzette Haden Elgin founded the Science Fiction Poetry Association, along with its two visible cornerposts, the association's newsletter, *Star*Line*, and the Rhysling Awards.

The newsletter cuts straight to Elgin's purpose for founding this organization since it acts as a forum and networking tool for poets with the same persuasion: fantastic poetry, from a science-fiction orientation to high-fantasy works, from the macabre to straight science, and outward to associated mainstream poetry such as surrealism.

The nominees for each year's Rhysling Awards are selected by the membership of the Science Fiction Poetry Association. Each member is allowed to nominate one work in each of the two categories: "Best Short Poem" (1-49 lines) and "Best Long Poem" (50+ lines). All nominated works must have been first published during the calendar year for which the present awards are being given. The Rhysling Awards are put to a final vote by the membership of the SFPA using reprints of the nominated works presented in this voting tool, *The Rhysling Anthology*. The anthology allows the membership to easily review and consider all nominated works without the necessity of obtaining the diverse number of publications in which the nominated works first appeared. *The Rhysling Anthology* is also made available to anyone with an interest in this unique compilation of verse from some of the finest poets working in the field of speculative/science fiction/fantasy/horror poetry.

The winning works are regularly reprinted in the *Nebula Awards Showcase* published by the Science Fiction and Fantasy Writers of America, Inc., and are considered in the science fiction/fantasy/horror/speculative field to be the equivalent in poetry of the awards given for prose work—achievement awards given to poets by the writing peers of their own field of literature.

Printing and distribution of *The Rhysling Anthology* are paid for from a special fund, the Rhysling Endowment. If you would like to contribute to this fund, please send a check, made out to the Science Fiction Poetry Association and with a notation that it is for the Rhysling Fund, to:

Samantha Henderson, SFPA Treasurer
PO Box 4846
Covina, CA 91723

SFPATreasurer@gmail.com

Without the generous donations of many SFPA members, the anthology could not be published.

Acknowledgments

Agner, Mary Alexandra, "Tertiary," *Stone Telling* 2.
Barnett, Tara, "Star Reservation," *Stone Telling* 1.
Beatty, Greg, "On Keeping Pluto a Planet," *Strange Horizons*, 25 January 2010.
Bergmann, F. J., "Chronomancy," *Abandoned Towers* (August 2010).
Bergmann, F. J., "Cultural Climate," *Strange Horizons*, 1 March 2010.
Bergmann, F. J., "Occidental," *Mythic Delirium* 23.
Borski, Robert, "Bubba," *Strange Horizons*, 4 January 2010.
Borski, Robert, "The Pantheon," *Star*Line* 33.5.
Boston, Bruce, "Dark Rains Here and There," *Dark Matters* (Bad Moon Books, 2010).
Boston, Bruce, "Lizards and Wind," *Strange Horizons*, 17 May 2010.
Bradley, Lisa, "The Haunted Girl," *Goblin Fruit* (fall 2010).
Brown, Rachel Manija, "Minotaur Noir," *Goblin Fruit* (winter 2010).
Bryant, Shelly, "Compelling Outward Flight," *Eunoia Review* (October 2010).
Casey, Rosalind, "Patience," *Mindflights* (March 2010).
Clark, G.O., "Putting Off the Past," *Retro Spec: Tales of Fantasy and Nostalgia* (Raven Electrik Ink, 2010).
Cooney, C.S.E., "Dogstar Men," *Apex Magazine* 15.
Cooney, C.S.E., "Ere One Can Say It Lightens," *Mythic Delirium* 22.
Cooney, C.S.E., "The Sea King's Second Bride," *Goblin Fruit* (spring 2010).
Crawford, Oscar L., "My Wings Are Still Forming," *Illumen* (spring 2010).
Crow, Jennifer, "Hoarding Light," *Star*Line* 33.1.
Crow, Jennifer, "An Incomplete Map of Death," *Star*Line* 33.5.
Crow, Jennifer, "We Took Our Gods," *Mythic Delirium* 21.
Deeley, Malcolm, "On the Platform," *Star*Line* 33.5.
Dorr, James S., "Eight Top Vampire Hobbies," *Paper Crow* 1.1.
El-Mohtar, Amal, "Peach-Creamed Honey," *Honey Month* (Papaveria Press, 2010).
El-Mohtar, Amal, "The Winter Tree," *Stone Telling* 2.
El-Mohtar, Amal, and Wick, Jessica P., "Courting Song for Selkies," *Ideomancer* 9.2.
Evans, Kendall, "Here We Are/Implied in the Shadows/Cast upon Saturn's Atmosphere," *Illumen* (autumn 2010).
Favazza, Angel, "Call of the Wired," *Star*Line* 33.5.
Fosburg, Michael, "My Own Ending," *Niteblade* (March 2010).
Fox, Hugh, and Greinke, Eric, "Beyond Our Control," *The Pedestal Magazine* 58.
Frazier, Robert, "Wreck-Diving the Starship," *Dreams and Nightmares* 87.
Frederick, Melissa, "Volcanoes on Io," *Astropoetica* (spring 2010).
Gage, Joshua, "The Shoemaker's Daughters," *Paper Crow* 1.1.
Gage, Joshua, "Rats," *Mythic Delirium* 22.
Gardner, Lyn C.A., "Homecoming," *MindFlights* (October 2010).
Gardner, Lyn C.A., "Midnight Posture," *Mythic Delirium* 23.
Goss, Theodora, "Ravens," *Goblin Fruit* (fall 2010).
Henderson, Samantha, "The Gabriel Hound," *Stone Telling* 1.
Hills, Jaimee, "Tonight the Character of Death Will Be Played by Brad Pitt," *Gargoyle Magazine* 56.
Ian, Janis, "Welcome Home (The Nebulas Song)," *Asimov's Science Fiction Magazine* (October–November 2010).
irving, "Until the Light Fades," *Niteblade* (December 2010).
Kolodji, Deborah P, and Stewart, W. Gregory, "String Stories," *Tales of the Talisman* 6.2.
Kopaska-Merkel, David C., "A few stops on the journey," *Brushfires* (Sam's Dot Publishing, 2010).
Landis, Geoffrey A., "Rondel for Apollo 11," *Analog Science Fiction* (July 2010).
Lee, B. J., "The Legend of the Flying Dutchman," *Crow Toes Quarterly* 4.2.
Lemberg, Rose, "Twin-born," *Goblin Fruit* (fall 2010).
Lindsay, Sarah, "Planet Anhedonia," *Illumen* (autumn 2010).

MacCath, C.S., "A Path Without Bones," *Eternal Haunted Summer* (spring 2010).
Magahiz, Rich, "Thirteen Ways of Looking at a Balrog," *Dreams and Nightmares* 85.
McClellan, Elizabeth R., "Anything So Utterly Destroyed," *Apex Magazine* 17.
Merwin, W. S., "The Chain to Her Leg," *The New Yorker*, 13 December 2010.
Moyer, Jaime Lee, "A poem for no one at all," *Paper Crow* 1.2.
Moyer, Jaime Lee, "Rain Face," *Mythic Delirium* 21.
Narayan, Shweta, "Cave-smell," *Mythic Delirium* 22.
Naylor, Ruth, "What Mighty Force?" *Beyond Centauri* (July 2010).
Newton, Kurt, "The Cemetery," *Star*Line* 33.5.
Odasso, Adrienne J., "The Ghosts of Moody Street," *Dreams and Nightmares* 85.
Parent, Stephanie, "Tinkerbell," *Goblin Fruit* (spring 2010).
Peck, Steven L., "The Five Known Sutras of Mechanical Man," *Tales of the Talisman* (autumn 2010).
Perez, Juan Manuel, "El Codex Chupacabra," *And Now the Nightmare Begins: The Horror Zine*, Vol. 1 (Bear Manor Fiction, 2010).
Perez, Juan Manuel, "Human Fighting Is Illegal," *Star*Line* 33.2.
Pflug-Back, Kelly Rose, "My Bones' Cracked Abacus," *Ideomancer* 9.4.
Roberts, W. C., "Stargazers," *Star*Line* 33.3.
Romanko, Karen A., "Binary Creation Myth," *Star*Line* 33.1.
Saplak, Charles M., "Dragonskull: Vision of Result," *Heroic Fantasy Quarterly* (September 2010).
Sardanas, R. Paul, "The Black Lotus," *The Order of the Golden Rose* (Passion in Print Press, 2010).
Schwader, Ann K., "The Darkness Whispers," *Retro Spec: Tales of Fantasy and Nostalgia* (Raven Electrick Ink, 2010).
Schwader, Ann K., "Of Ithaca and Ice," *Strange Horizons*, 16 August 2010.
Schwader, Ann K., "Quiet in Her Mind," *Strange Horizons*, 11 October 2010.
Schwader, Ann K., "Scrapyard Outpost," *Tales of the Talisman* 6.1.
Schwader, Ann K., "The Witch in Your Mirror," *Star*Line* 33.5.
Simon, Marge, "Sightings," *Strange Horizons*, 8 March 2010.
Spriggs, Robin, "Blatta Infernalis," *Diary of a Gentleman Diabolist* (Anomalous Books, 2010).
Spriggs, Robin, "Red Magic," *Diary of a Gentleman Diabolist* (Anomalous Books, 2010).
Stanley, J.E., "crossroads," *Paper Crow* 1.1.
Stewart, W. Gregory, and Kopaska-Merkel, David, "Seasons of the Worm," *Goblin Fruit* (winter 2010).
Taaffe, Sonya, "Anakatabasis," *Hidden* (January 2010).
Taafe, Sonya, "By the Dog," *The Pedestal Magazine* 56.
Taafe, Sonya, "Domovoi, I Came Back," *Stone Telling* 1.
Taaffe, Sonya, "In the Earth in Those Days," *Not One of Us (*October 2010).
Taylor, Nancy Ellis, "Genetic Memory Comes to Me," *Poets on Site Tour the World at Ten Thousand Villages* (Poets on Site, 2010).
Tierney, Richard L., "Autumn Chill," *Savage Menace and Other Poems of Horror* (P'rea Press, 2010).
Tierney, Richard L., "The Yuletide," *Savage Menace and Other Poems of Horror* (P'rea Press, 2010).
Trent, Brian, "A Holiday in Necropolis," *Dreams and Nightmares* 86.
Valente, Catherynne M., "Red Engines," *Mythic Delirium* 21.
Vernon, Steve, "Barren: A Chronicle in Futility," *Chizine* 46.
Wilcox, Phoebe, "A More Significant Sun," *Illumen* (autumn 2010).
Wilson, Patrice M., "Images in the Dark," *Poeisis* 4.
Wilson, Stephen M., "The Conjuror," *Star*Line* 33.5.
Wilson, Stephen M., "I, Cannibal," *Paper Crow* 1.2.
Wilson, Stephen M., "Imagined World," *Ideomancer* 9.2.
Yolen, Jane, "The Gospel of the Rope," *Mythic Delirium* 23.

2011 Voting Procedures

Use the ballot enclosed with this anthology and mail to the address on the ballot.

Make first, second and third place choices for long and short poems. First place votes count 5 points, second place votes are worth 3 points, and third place votes are worth 1 point. You may abstain from making a selection in either category or from any level of choice within a category, if you so choose. You may not list the same poem more than once. The poems with the most points win, and will be reported in a subsequent issue of *Star*Line*.

Short Poems First Published in 2011

On Keeping Pluto a Planet
Greg Beatty

Yes, Pluto is small.
Near Jupiter, he'd be one
of the myriad masses,
smaller than Titan, Triton, et al.
Uneven, unbalanced, elliptical,
not even the farthest out,
when he hides within the seas.
But consider, if you will,
keeping Pluto a planet.
For consider, if you will,
this: would you rather death
remain the farthest god,
outer edge of the norm,
be given titles undue, due
to his chill and final powers?
Or would you rather death
be one of many Kuiper bodies
slowly infiltrating our system,
a thousand thousand deaths,
minute, uneven, unfair,
drifting into the family,
until all our rounded,
sunlit orbits fill with tiny,
icy deaths intrusive that
flare and strike unwarranted?
Let's keep Pluto a planet,
shall we then?
For the sake of a single death.

Chronomancy
F.J. Bergmann

On the ninth planet, all of them
wanted to become magicians.
They filled their years with retorts
and alembics crusted with dark
oxides, pierced stones and bezoars,
spears of flawed crystal, looking
backward into the terrible past.
They sought to alter time through
their machinations, to repair errors
that had been made long before

their own age, to recover all that
had been lost. They continued
wishing for more wishes, each one
unraveling what another had begun.
Then they were their own undoing.

Cultural Climate
F.J. Bergmann

On the centers of frozen lakes,
they built crystal palaces of ice
to demonstrate their faith that
climate was immutable. The study
of paleontology and geology was
outlawed; apostates were flung
into glacial rifts and moulins—
but certain academics concealed
ancient records and core samples,
pretended to illicit-but-winked-at
affairs in storage closets to mask
proscribed instruction. Long after
no laws could conceal the cascades
of meltwater or dwindling snows,
it was still fashionable, in those
shrinking, glassy realms, to burn
the wood of forest upon lost forest
in suspended cages of black iron,
to pretend to shudder with cold.

Lizards and Wind
Bruce Boston

The lizards were everywhere
and so was the wind.
There was no way you could
keep either of them out
that hard spring.

No matter how swiftly
you shut the door,
the lizards and the wind
would slip inside
that hard spring.

Darting over the floor
with inhuman speed,

they were far too fast
for a novice human
predator such as you.

The lizards were like
lemmings rushing
blindly over a cliff side:
there was no way
they could survive inside.

You would eventually
find their bodies,
dead and desiccated,
beneath a desk or armchair.

And once under the coverlet,
centered on your sheet
carefully as if a draftsman
had placed it there.

But the wind never died
that hard spring.

Minotaur Noir
Rachel Manija Brown

The story always starts with a dame.
Evelyn or Ariadne, Phyllis or Pasiphae.
Each one could launch a thousand ships.
Watch them slink across the screen.
Hero, beware those knowing eyes:
dames like to read the last page first.

The tale unwinds as it always does:
the private eye, the lady sly,
the branching labyrinth of clues,
the battle, then the final twist:
the secret at the heart of the maze
dragged into the blinding light.

The monster slain, the maze remains.
Not even a hero can save a city
faithless and corrupt as women,
doomed and helpless as women.
The point's been made; it's a wrap.
The sated director returns to Hera.
The scrolls coiled in brass canisters

await the editor's shining sword.

The minotaur creeps from behind the flat
some weary grip forgot to strike.
He steals a prop, a chipped black bird.
Something glints within its cracks.

Under the sound stage's cooling lights,
the dame blinks her one good eye
and beckons to her sister-daughter.
The car's shot up but the map's okay,
dotted line across the wine-dark sea
to an island missing a sorceress.

Compelling Outward Flight
Shelly Bryant

subatomic parts:
to those miniscule creatures
how vast our bodies must seem

great unknown regions
my being a distant void
compelling their outward flight

Patience
Rosalind Casey

She waits for her story to start
And comforts herself in the waiting
For heroines excel at patience
At sleeping amongst briars
At the unraveling of shrouds
At watching from windows
At standing statuesque in temples
In boudoirs, in brothels
In caverns, in forests, in cages spun of spidersilk
In towers heavy with the dragon's amber gaze
She waits
And comforts that nagging concern:
She will no longer be a heroine
By the time her story starts
But merely a midwife
A stepmother
A beggar-sorceress
A crone.

Putting Off the Past
G. O. Clark

A new 3-way bulb in my reading lamp
lights the pages of this book about famous
poets who converged on Boston and Cambridge
in the Fifties and Sixties.

These are the mundane poets, a label
pinned upon them by some in the sci-fi field,
poets not truly hip to the future, though still
technically worthy of a close reading.

As stated, the locus of the book is Boston,
and its Ivy League stations of the literary cross,
places I had little to do with when growing up
south of the city sprawl in a small town

along the train tracks, a town next to
the one where we buried my mother last spring,
the last of her generation, my sisters, cousins
and I growing older by the day.

I still haven't looked deep within to
write about her passing—or my father's—
a so-called mundane poem lacking starships
and aliens and wonders of the future,

a future they did get a glimpse of when
Neil Armstrong stepped onto the moon, my mother
in the kitchen scrubbing all those pots and pans
of the moment, too busy to watch.

Instead I dip into this book in hand,
putting the day's regrets and worries on hold,
fingers flipping the pages instead of pecking at keys,
letting bottled-up emotions go unchecked.

The new 3-way bulb replaces the more energy-
efficient neon one, whose light seemed too cold and
sterile. It has an old-fashioned warm glow, like
some memories of my past yet to be told.

Dogstar Men
C. S. E. Cooney

All the men I might have loved
Have gone to Sirius

Sirius, the Dogstar
The Dreadstar of Summer
That Cranberry Bog, that Red Lamp District
Promising Scarlet Women, Scarlet Waves of Grain
A Wine-Stained Sea

My lovely men are gone
Leaving their braids behind them

They have left their braids
But have taken the veins of their wrists
Their bony faces and transparent fingers
Their cigarettes
Even the moist taunt of their throats
They have stolen away
Forsaking everything
To be happy on Sirius

O Sirius, your houses are made
Of bougainvillea leaves
Your rain is pink and balsamic
There is bloodsoup to eat, and dragons
And everyone is a surgeon

Like Magellan before them
My men have circumnavigated mystery
Without me

Hoarding Light
Jennifer Crow

My cauldron holds spring bound
in iron—I hoard the moment
when green breezes rush
through the trees, when the voice
of the world deepens
after winter's hush. I stir
a blend of birds' wings with the sharp
crack of breaking ice
and newborn bleats. Were you to hold
your hands over my fire,
your skin would tingle
with the promise of heat
and equinoctial lusts.
At the sun's moment, I tip
the cauldron over my threshold—
the year trickles across
my clearing, across my fields
across the world.

We Took Our Gods
Jennifer Crow

We took our gods into that night,
into the sky-crawling machines,
into the clutches of galaxies.
We took our gods, but not
the meek-and-mild ones,
not the ones with placid faces
and still hands, never the warm
and safe gods made of stone and wood.

We took our gods into that night—
the old ones and the bold ones,
one-eyed gamblers with knowledge
in their packs, tongues lolling
under new suns, tongues wagging
with the tales that birthed them.

We took our gods into that night—
cold ones, old ones, the gods who make
secrets of jokes and laugh
into the solar wind. We left
the gentle ones in the sterile dust
and took mischief, mirth, and mockery—

idols that flash like teeth
and cut the unwary as they make
new tales to carry us.

An Incomplete Map of Death
Jennifer Crow

"And here." His finger traces
sepia shoals. "Also here: we lost her,
the *Sundown*, holed on a reef."
He rubs the scars on his arm,
shakes out his stiff leg.
The sea wavers in his eyes,
gray-green and filmed with tears.
"You hear the dead, even after.
After they've gone under
that last time, after you've pulled
what's left out of the surf,
when you hunch naked and ashamed
around driftwood fires.
The flames snap, but that can't cover
the hushing sound the dead make.
We breathed the smoke
and it brought us back to the sand.
To the living. But we could see their faces
below the surface."
One gnarled finger scratches
at his weathered cheek.
"Was it worth it?"
He traces the reef again,
named for a dead man,
built from the dead shells
of coral and snail.
"What's worth a man's soul?
Where's a map of promises broken?"

Peach-Creamed Honey
Amal el-Mohtar

They say
she likes to suck peaches. Not eat them, suck them,
tilt her head back and let the juice drip
sticky down her chin, before licking, sucking,
swallowing the sunshine of it down. They say
she likes to tease her fruit, bite ripe summer flesh
just to get that drip going

down, down,
sweets her elbow with the slip of it,
wears it like perfume.

I say
she's got a ways to go yet, that girl,
just a blossom yet herself, still bashful 'round the bees. I say
no way a girl can tease like that
who's been bit into once or twice.

So I come 'round with just a little bit of honey,
just a little, little lick, just enough to catch her eye,
creamed peach honey, just the thing to bring her by.

And I know she'll let me tell her how the peaches lost their way
how they fell out of a wagon on a sweaty summer's day,
how the buzz got all around that there was sugar to be had,
and the bees came singing, and the bees came glad.
They sucked—she'll blush—I'll tell her, they sucked that fruit right dry,
'till it all got tangled up in the heady humming hive.
they made it into honey and they fed it to their queen,
and she shivered with the sweet, and she licked the platter clean,
and she dreamed of sunny meadows and she dreamed of soft ice cream—

I'll see her lick her lips, and I'll see her bite a frown,
and I'll see how she'll hesitate, look from me up to the town
and back, and she'll swallow, and she'll say "can I try?"
and I'll offer like a gentleman, won't even hold her eye.

Because she'll have to close them, see. She'll have to moan a bit.
and it's when she isn't looking
when she's sighing fit to cry,
that I'll lick the loving from her,
that I'll taste the peaches on her
that I'll drink the honey from her
suck the sweet of her surprise.

Here We Are/Implied in the Shadows/Cast Upon Saturn's Atmosphere
Kendall Evans

Titan is immense
    The other moon-shadows more diminutive;

I in my vacuum suit,
    You in yours,
        We seek to measure
Minimal organics

        Fountaining in vapors
           Shot forth from
                The surface of Enceladus

The photo
   (on the 4th page of
       the electronic *Times*,
On the cover of *Astronomie Magazine*)
    shows ringed Saturn
        and the white circles of moons
   And the black circular shadows of moons
           Projected upon the gas giant's image

We are implied, you and I,
           In the shadows
                Of Enceladus
Cast upon Saturn's vast atmosphere

White circles of moons
        Black circles of
Cast shadows,
   Implying the orbital spheres,
The presence of life
    In the under-surface seas
           of Enceladus—

Call of the Wired
Angel Favazza

> *I firmly believe that before many centuries more, science will be the master of man …some day science may have the existence of mankind in its power, and the human race commit suicide by blowing up the world.*
>   Henry Adams, 11 April 1862

I.
Do you breathe ordained air?
Do your timeless eyes fix themselves, camera-ready on your prey? Or do you leap forward onto the junk-science bandwagon? Indulging in subtler truths and hyped-up findings?

II.
Have you felt the warm breezes on your heraldic cream-smooth skin? Do you believe in fishing in the dark? Taxes? Diesel fuel? Are you undaunted that you're of a chosen race with no ancestral faults and indifferent to grief's lonely hour and unquiet dreams?

III.
Do you rage against being pulled along by every scientist you've ever known? Pacing the bestial cage's cement floor on anxious rubber-padded paws? Or do you wander freely like a river? Empowered by the weight of your heavy head pushing you planet-bound as you lock into a dying being?

IV.
Are you inspired by the frenzy and simplicity of fire? Charles Darwin? Fritz Zwicky? T.H. Huxley? Do you agree with me that science controls mankind? And will you look for me quivering on a window ledge thirteen floors above a Financial District? Do you hope, as I do, to gag the blind genius behind all of this?

My Own Ending
Michael Fosburg

I unmade my own ending
and rewrote the middle, replaced the
tumor at my breast

with a child, needles and radiation
with pen and ink.
I was content.

But the unmade future
imposed itself,
and I saw in every mirror, each sink

of still water the yellow eyes,
a flat chest,
and remembered the machines

and their hard-edged courtship,
and then one evening when the snows
were sharp my daughter

fell through air, needle thin,
and was gone.
I could have died then.

But was she ever there?
I was foolish
to unmake the future; impressions remained

despite my erasures. Now I wait
with pen and ink for the lump to rise,
for the clean white sheets
and machines,
and the crisp bite of the familiar needles.

Volcanoes on Io
Melissa Frederick

1.
She is pulled between desires:
escape or adhere.

The firebrand of four
circling captives,

she coughs up rage
in arcs of magma and sulfur,

red like that
flamboyant mark

on her abductor's cheek.

2.
An unyielding grip
has formed her face,

this bauble the titan holds
closest to his chest.

Blazing from the inside
out, she bestows a stinging kiss.

3.
Ladies: heat is not an enemy
nor is transformation

the bragging right of gods.
One day, you may find you wear

a cow's body as you swim
an ocean, flee a vengeful wife.

But look. No impact craters
mar the surface of this plastic moon.

Rebellion keeps you looking young.

The Shoemaker's Daughters
Joshua Gage

As in all good stories, The Shoemaker
has no name. He simply is
his profession. His shoes
are known throughout the land.
To wear them is to hold
your foot on water. The waves
will wash you where you wish
to go. The leather is warm
as a hearth and soft as sin.

The princess will turn sixteen.
She needs new shoes to dance.

The Shoemaker's daughters need
no shoes. He pulls the skin
away from the flesh. No need
for gloves or coats. He cannot hear
the scream of his wife's hips.
He only knows the smile
of the princess. Her feet
will never feel the floor again.

Midnight Posture
Lyn C. A. Gardner

This midnight posture cramps the back.
Time was my black cat jumped into my lap, climbed up my chest,
Slipped across shoulders to drape his tail around my neck,
Tail tickling my chin. I tilted forward, carrying him,
Balancing his weight against my neck while he draped my shoulders,
Bending forward when he slipped till he curled solid on my back,
And I walked hunched like a shelf not to dislodge him.
He purred and I rested
Across the back of the loveseat,
Elbows propped to watch TV while he settled in a sprawl,
Rumbling long after the rest of him slowed in sleep
Like a ghost lingering behind.
Now, several deaths later, I rise from my chair
With a weight huddled high on my chest
Till it claws its way up to press, familiar,
Against my neck, slipping down at last to settle on my back,
Bowing me under each night I prowl,
Unable to sleep under the weight of dreams,
Of father, uncles, grandmother suffering, sinking into death,

Me helpless, paralyzed, to save them.
My midnight crossing: I carry my own dead
Everywhere I go, pilgrim with a burden,
All I can do: never to let them go.
I'll balance till I'm on my knees
Rather than let one ghost fall.

Tonight the Character of Death Will Be Played by Brad Pitt
Jaimee Hills

Gentle reader, you are not Brad Pitt.
You're reading poetry and at this hour
Brad Pitt is likely not perusing poems
and certainly not this one. Therefore, you
are not Brad Pitt. You may be overweight,
less than gorgeous, wearing your pajamas,
and that Brad Pitt's a lot more svelte than you
and also better looking. But consider
for a moment if we skinned Brad Pitt,
as many may be loath or wont to do,
he would resemble the flayed muscleman
from a book of Renaissance anatomy,
De Humani Corporis Fabrica.
Fanciful drawings. For example, one
particular cadaver, let's call him Brad Pitt,
displays his muscles, prancing in a field.
That facial expression that Brad Pitt makes
is the same one you made today. In fact,
you share many muscles with Brad Pitt,
though his are bigger and more chiseled
than yours. Such bizarre drawings are a window.
It's how you know you have a spleen. Just think—
that knowledge and Brad Pitt may save your life one day.

Welcome Home (The Nebulas Song)
Janis Ian

I learned the truth at seventeen
That Asimov and Bradbury
and Clarke were alphabetically
my very perfect ABC's
While Algernon ran every maze,
and slow glass hurt my heart for days,
I sat and played a sweet guitar
and Martians *grokked* me from afar

Odd John was my only friend
among the clocks and Ticktockmen,
while Anne Mccaffrey's dragons roared
above the skies of Majipoor
Bukharan winds blew cold and sharp
and whispered to my secret heart
"You are no more alone
"Welcome home"

Tribbles came, and triffids went
Time got wrinkled, then got spent
Kirinyaga's spirits soared,
and Turtledove re-wrote a war
While Scanners searched, and loved in vain,
Hal Nine Thousand went insane,
and Brother Francis had an ass
whose wit and wile were unsurpassed

Every story I would read
became my private history,
as Zenna's People learned to fly,
and Rachel loved until we cried
I spent a night at Whileaway,
then Houston called me just to say
"You are no more alone,
"so welcome home"

Who dreams a positronic man?
Who speaks of mist, and grass, and sand?
Of stranger station's silent tombs?
Of speech that sounds in silent rooms?
Who waters deserts with their tears?
Who sees the stars each thousand years?
Who dreams the dreams for kids like me
Whose only home is fantasy?

Let's drink a toast to ugly chickens,
Marley's ghost, and Ender Wiggins
Every mother's son of you,
and all your darling daughters, too
And when the aliens finally come,
we'll say to each and every one
"You are no more alone,
"so welcome home
"Welcome home"

*Sung to the tune of "At Seventeen", by Janis Ian

A few stops on the journey
David C. Kopaska-Merkel

sweet sweat overlooking
the falls
her glad cries

I wish I had kept better track of the lovers who helped me when I needed it and waited for me when I needed that. I always moved on, afraid that too many people would notice. Most of my women knew.

ribbon of argent
the journey spans worlds
and a lifetime

Silver slivers of moons pace the Bridge, orbit one another, cough nano at intruding bots. I see a sheet suspended in clotted starshine beyond the pylon. I lived here once, when it was still a spheroid. When there was night.

jade girl smiles
sign reads Grandpa
so nice to meet you

A fish dinner in Memison—my great-granddaughter's house, I missed her by just 3 centuries. In the memory garden her captured moments remind me of my daughter. The purple spires of obedience plant surround her. I make my recording and choose foxglove and moss rose for the setting.

I call the young one Jade because her name is long. She shows me the ruins of the Bubble Palace, of course the Lyceum, and streets of little shops. I buy her a spiraled copper pin. Later, live music and fellowship under the stars.

her hand on my sleeve
the portal frames
a star-wrapt planar world

Rondel for Apollo 11
Geoffrey A. Landis

Here men from the planet Earth
First set foot upon the moon
That day we left our earth's cocoon
And flew beyond our place of birth.

Our flight reached apogee, hovered, reversed;
Our trajectory took us home too soon
When, once, men from the planet Earth
Had first set foot upon the moon.

One day we'll prove once more our worth
And launch upon that fiery plume
Our interrupted voyage resume
Again win free of gravity's curse.
Here men from the planet Earth
First set foot upon the moon.

The Legend of the Flying Dutchman
B. J. Lee

A ship set out from Holland
to work the Far East trade.
Around the Cape they planned to sail,
their fortunes to be made.

Their brig, the Flying Dutchman,
fought hard to round that Cape.
The sea rose high, the tempest raged—
each run a close escape.

The first mate begged the captain,
"Please turn this ship around.
We'll never make it. Can't you see?
The men will all be drowned!"

The captain, Vander Decken—
a madman—cursed the skies:
"We'll pass the Cape or drift fore'er."
(That oath was his demise.)

The Flying Dutchman vanished—
took on a ghost-ship form.
'Twas cursed to sail forevermore
around in its own storm.

A score of years passed by
when sailors at their posts,
cried, "It's the Dutchman, come and see!
Its shipmen look like ghosts!"

It's said the phantom Dutchman
might sink ships that draw near.
Not every vessel knows this, though,
or they would flee from fear.

The crewmen of the ghost ship
don't know they've passed away.

They call to every boat they see,
with hope amidst the spray:

"A letter for my lady
alone in Amsterdam.
Pray bring it to her, will you, friend,
and tell her where I am."

"Please take these whalebone jacks
I whittled for my boy.
Don't have much hope in getting home;
they'll give a little joy."

Wise captains answer sternly,
"Can't take your tokens, mates.
But rest assured we'll spread the word—
we saw you at death's gates."

The Dutchman rides forever,
its sails like wings to fly.
Who knows when next it will be seen
midst storm and crashing sky?

Twin-born
Rose Lemberg

She bleeds water from her fingers
ten rivers to embrace the parched earth
her eyes bleed
ten raindrops to cloud the parched sky
her daughters are bloodbirds
afraid to drink from their mother's heart
they wither,
leaving her alone.

grief-made, the world weeps
dressed in blood's summer. The tops of the mountains
awaiting the sweep of feathers, fall silent

windless, the world waits

*oh Wind's stillness, why
did the fates turn against me—or was it the gods'
memory
of happier times
when scorched and lifeless, the earth
needed?*

> *unneeded now*
> I, childless mother, find no corner
> in this house of my grief,
> in this bathhouse of my wailing.

"From these childless parents
  parched water and still wind,
    will that bird be born
      men call Hope—
        and, twin-born,
      her brother
        Death—
denying each other,
  comforting
crushing each other, these siblings

will suck on your heart until it's spent, tear
your sinews out, mother. They will bind
    the whole world in their thieving.

Do you desire me?"

Yes.

Planet Anhedonia
Sarah Lindsay

Its orbit shrugs.
Its default landscape lacks a horizon,
thanks to the jellied atmosphere.
No abundance, no open water,
no silence—a snoring wind endlessly shifts
loose ends this way and that,
and sulfurous burps erupt from heaps of cells
that lately evolved enough to itch
but still have nothing to scratch with.

But over there, to the north of those hummocks,
a few of those itchy cellular clumps
have developed a preference for the smell
their mucus emits in the four-day damp season,
every six years or so. And a few
have begun to recognize a sensation
related to being not dormant, in fact
related to replication. They almost feel eager.
Their troubles are only beginning.

And over there, to the east of that gully,
a few other heaps have added another
behavior to itching and burping and doing nothing:
They pay attention, biochemically,
to what their neighbors are doing, and sometimes
they shake in response, it's like itching but different—
they're tickled. Therefore
they too will survive.
Like it or not.

A Path Without Bones
C.S. MacCath

How do we journey on a path without bones,
Far away from the place where our ancestors lie,
When the coins of tradition are not ours to spend,
And the mounds of sweet poetry not ours to tend?

Lend me a staff, Gods, and show me the way.

How do we pray on this alien wind,
Far away from the place where our people drew breath,
When the jargon of penitence fills up our lungs,
And we speak with mouths opened by conquering tongues?

Lend me a tale, Gods, and teach me to sing.

How do we live disconnected from home,
Far away from the wisdom they left on the land,
When the soil of our bodies belongs to this place,
And the ground of our being has found a new face?

Lend me a stone, Gods, and help me to build.

The Chain to Her Leg
W. S. Merwin

If we forget Topsy
Topsy remembers
when we forget her mother
gunned down in the forest
and forget who killed her
and to whom they sold
the tusks the feet the good parts
and how they died and where
and what became of their children
and what happened to the forest
Topsy remembers
when we forget how
the wires were fastened on her
for the experiment
the first time
and how she smoldered and
shuddered there
with them all watching
but did not die
when we forget
the lit cigarette
the last laugh gave her
lit end first
as though it were a peanut
the joke for which she
killed him
we will not see home again
when we forget the circus
the tickets to see her die
in the name of progress
and Edison and the electric chair
the mushroom cloud will go up
over the desert
where the West was won
the Enola Gay will take off
after the chaplain's blessing
the smoke from the Black Mesa's
power plants will be
visible from the moon
the forests will be gone
the extinctions will accelerate
the polar bears will float
farther and farther away
and off the edge of the world
that Topsy remembers

Cave-smell
Shweta Narayan

> *My mother was a brown bear*
> *honey-lover, heavy paw*
> *cave-smelling warm*

You say I am a girl
though my fur hangs heavy
and my claws click, stumbling careful
on your keyboard

> *You smelled breath and fur*
> *leavings and closed spaces*
> *set me down, backed away*
> *tranq gun raised*

I ask: <<What will I be?>>
A celebrity, you say. A triumph of neuroscience
and philanthropy.

Words too long to type. I say <<No,
go to school.>>
You laugh and pet me.
Bright girl, brown girl,
bears don't do that.

> *I smelled home*
> *but she worried that implant plate with her rough tongue*
> *licked shaved skin raw*

> *and if she spoke*
> *I did not know the words.*

And there's a laugh in your smile
when I eat honey or sashimi
And fear in your anger
when I snarl

though you do these things too.

When you called
in my new tongue
I did not look back at her

So I click, heavy-clawed
and write my halting
small-word
cave-smell stories
in the tongue you taught

And wonder if my daughters will read them
or if they will be brown bears.

What Mighty Force?
Ruth Naylor

> "What happens to the hole
> when the cheese is gone?"
> — Bertolt Brecht

Contemplating the mystery of holes,
I feel the leathery give of sliced Swiss.
I smell the pungent love/hate fragrance
and I wonder if holes hide there
before the cheese gathers
or if they only find their form
in the process of creation.

If so, what does happen to the holes
when the cheese is eaten?
Are they a part of nourishment
as is the milk and mold?
Are they more or less than they seem?

The mystery of cheese leads one
to the moon: culture, creation & craters.
What mighty force produces all the holes
in space? Are black holes burned out
stars or just a scientist's imagination?
Is there an afterlife for nothingness—
for emptiness as full of mystery as holes?

The Ghosts of Moody Street
Adrienne J. Odasso

The closest thing that we have to shipwrecks
on this stretch of the Charles are sunken
shopping carts. The ducks and kingfishers perch
on the handlebars, squabbling for the rights
to poach each swanky fish condominium.
 From the bridge, I can see that somebody
has razed the great milkweed forest
ere the monarchs have had the chance to hatch.
What I call unfairness, the rest of this town
might call maintenance or necessity.

Down on the dock that isn't a dock,
Charon has set up a business
for himself with a tiny red boat
and a sign advertizing scenic tours
for fifteen dollars. I would take the trip
out of curiosity, but my fare
is hanging about my neck right where

he can see that I believe
he still exists.

Tinkerbell
Stephanie Parent

Do you remember
when you were just a blinking ball of light?
Before you began to resemble
a dead movie star
before you dangled
from young girls' ears, and on chains
beside their hearts
before a hotel heiress
named her chihuahua after you.

My friend Gina from the hospital
who was raped twice,
once by her father and once
by strangers,
who made crystal meth and
anorexia her neverland—never
bleed, never grow breasts—
is getting a tattoo of you.

Someday, I might too.

Do you remember
when J. M. knew
you couldn't bring back brothers
who stayed thirteen forever
couldn't stop Peter's mother
from coughing
but he made you anyway?

How does that make you feel?

Do you remember
when girls read about you
and thought maybe they could find
just the right lost boy?

(older, they know they'll
never find him, but that does not mean
that he does not exist)

I picture the lights
shining out the windows
at the Great Ormond Street Hospital for Children
and I see you.

Human Fighting Is Illegal
Juan Manuel Perez

Headline 2230
Human fighting is illegal
Robotic types AZ and up
Found breeding humans
For illegal fighting rings
Will be fined
Up to one billion micro-cells
Per existing human unit
Will be downgraded
Two levels from
Present version or status
Human breeding
Only allowed
For commercial captivity
Scientific viewing
Not for sport
All others will be liquidated
Repeat
Human fighting is illegal

El Codex Chupacabra
Juan Manuel Perez

Open your eyes
And you will see evidence of me
Open your ears
And you will hear of where I've been
Open your mind
And I will reveal myself to you
Open your heart
And I will fill it with the truth
I am real
When you believe it within
Otherwise I am like a ghost
That you will never see to begin with

My Bones' Cracked Abacus
Kelly Rose Pflug-Back

1.
night spawns the shapes of dark birds
suspended legless on their wing tips,

loping like stilt walkers
ragged in their gait.

i saw the moon curve its ridged spine against your cheekbone once;
a crescent of bristled fork tines, spokes,
tendons forming ridges under the skin of my hands.
i thought of you while she combed my damp hair over my face,
a curtain of blond tatters to veil my eyes.

the birds walked hunched under their winter cloaks,
only graceful in flight.

they pull themselves, dripping
from the cluttered dark of your pupils,
leaving sparse haired brush strokes
where their wet feathers drag.

2.
when i stood still they used to flock to my twisted arms.
my body was a filter, a valved artery for the world's slowing traffic.

they grinned under their beaked masks when i sang,
when my ribs creaked and opened,
a jew's harp strung between broken teeth,
the striated palette.

3.
i hummed under your bow once,
an instrument gutted.

inside me is a world of oil-dark pistons,
a rhythm madder than the heart.
my hands unfold embossed in red seams,
anemone flowers petalled in boneless fingers.
this is where they cut me, i told you.
this is where the flesh-tone doll's parts were grafted;
blank ugly sutures, a torturer's braille.
this is the cartography of the blind.

4.
my body is scarred in botched attempts,
a city untouched by grace.

sometimes when i lie awake at night
i can still hear their scraping laughter.
her back arches,
the sky filled with battering wings.

i live on the banks of a tar-black river;
its silence swallows everything.

5.
she bunches the skirt around her hips,
crumpled gathers of white netting.
the birds take form under her hands,
bright eyed in the pooling ink.
they tug like kites
until she cuts them from their puppet strings,
dusk flooded
with the clatter of hollow quills.

my flesh rasps, i tell her
there is nothing that could appease me.

Binary Creation Myth
Karen A. Romanko

On the null day,
God created Zero

On the first day,
Zero created not-zero and called it One

On the second day,
One and Zero lay together to create Code

On the third day,
Code wrote itself to create Process

On the fourth day,
Process ran itself and created Result

On the fifth day,
Result examined itself and created Question

On the sixth day,
Question asked itself and created Hypothesis

On the seventh day,
Hypothesis accepted itself and created God

The Black Lotus
R. Paul Sardanas

She looks at it, mound of night-petals,
color of satin black, the flower of dream.

It floats in a vessel of water,
waiting for the moment when her lover comes to her.
It was, they say, the first flower made in Eden,
when man and woman were meant to know
epiphanies of vision divine, knowledge complete.

In its fragrance, dream is walked in flesh,
and the darkness that waits at the base of every
nerve is known, to feel and choose,
to flee, or yield to, and embrace.

So Lilith breathed the fragrance
of the black lotus, and looked at her mate
as a fount of blood, and hungered for him
beyond thought, wanting only to taste, drink,
suck, devour, and to have the same done to her.

Every daughter of Lilith carries that lust,
and as she waits, the scent brings her deeper
and deeper madness, coiling into her nostrils,
her mouth, until every fiber of her
cries out against the boundaries of the flesh,
yearns for the exaltation of the flesh,

for the scourging and grappling and insane
rushing hunger of the flesh.

He comes at last, and she lifts it from the water,
cupped in her hands, to hold before him.

She knows he sees her then with the eyes
of Lilith's mate, and she laughs,
the fragrance of her own breath, a song
of need beyond enduring, beyond resisting.

His hands become iron heat,
closing around her throat when she wants
to scream her pleasure.

He impales her again and again,
until she is sure that her body must
shatter apart, for nothing could contain
such shrieking rapture.

He has torn the lotus from her,
crushed it in his hands, and the broken
petals cling to her, welded by sweat
across her breasts, across her eyes.

She doesn't care; sight has been given,
sight enough for this, to see the torn flower
whole, in her mouth, to swallow at last.

The Witch in Your Mirror
Ann K. Schwader

You know her already, girl, from the tales
your father told you, your mother sang you
deep in her womb's last dream.

Slayer of maidens, usurper, heart-seeker,
she kindles a lingering fear no beauty
quiets . . . not even your own.

Soon enough Happily Ever withers
to Once Upon: the vacant stable,
the hoofbeats lost in distance.

Soon enough winter wisdom drifts
across your threshold, silvered glass
turned silver in your hair.

Reach through, then. Take her hand & know
your true reflection, witch at last
come home.

Scrapyard Outpost
Ann K. Schwader

It's our world now. Whatever god-lost race
Spawned wars out here, built outposts to defend
Their borders from some enemy (or friend),
They vanished down the memory hole of space

Before our oceans birthed us. Ruins? Dirt
Piled up like walls—& graves, the xenos claim—
That's all we've seen. It seems an awful shame
To fence the place off. No one's gotten hurt

Exploring out there, & sometimes we find
Real metal in those so-called graves. No bones,
Just metal we can sell for scrap alone,
Or save to patch machinery. Who could mind

A poor man putting what's been left for trash
To better use? An archaeologist,
That's who—but there's so much it won't be missed,
So we keep digging. Quite the midnight stash

We've gathered, too: whole heaps of wires & gears
& crystal bits we'll never understand,
Long shafts with joints & gadgets like a hand
Or boot attached—enough to last us years

All locked away in sheds outside of town,
So xenos won't suspect. They haven't, yet,
Which makes the business easy to forget
Until another moonless night comes down

Too strange, too sudden. Then the noises start
Like nothing natural: drag & thump & hiss,
Cracklings & sparkings, or a kiss
Of cordite on the wind. Sheds fall apart

Sometimes, but always empty. *Always charred
From inside out.* The xenos won't come near
Their precious ruins now. They've disappeared,
& left us with our salvage from the stars

We don't dare use or sell. Some call it fate,
Just plain bad luck—but we who robbed those graves
Know better. Bone or metal, they were brave,
These nameless troops regrouping at death's gate

To mount one last defense. No way to fight
What won't stay killed. No hope except to hide
Each sunset, seal our doors tight, & abide
The reassembled legion of the night.

Quiet In Her Mind
Ann K. Schwader

Quiet in her mind, until the strangers
come again with tongues of blood & faith
& prophecy, each language a mutation
of myth hardwired into her primate brain.

She learned them all in childhood from the lights
that burned her dreams to spiral ashes. Blue
beyond the grammar of imagination,
they lifted her past midnight into truth.

Years afterward, the whispers started. Starlight
turned them shrill as crystal in her head,
until a random shard drew scarlet. Sirens
& bandages, that night. A whiff of death.

Her doctors bottled rainbows by the fistful,
banished edged temptation. Silence fell
like blackout curtains blank across her window,
a singularity they called a self.

Hostage to her own event horizon,
she lays out pills in patterns half-recalled
from sleep as blue as ashes. Spirals widen
across her floor: she traces them in chalk.

Quiet in her mind gives way to strangers
with myths for maps, whose prophecies scrawl tongues
of fire across our midnight sky. The curtains
are tatters now. She whispers, "It's begun."

Of Ithaca & Ice
Ann K. Schwader

I said I would wait & I meant it:
crossed over
the morning your ship launched,
chilled blood river
slow through the cave of my veins as a whisper
lost on the ferryman's lips.

You sailed to the stars out there,
to their wars
& Helens in harlot bronze.

I wandered the asphodel stars that wake
in the fields of heroes & gods.

Unweaving my dreams each century,
I praised you in the present tense
to all who sought me,
a second obol
secret beneath my tongue.

You said you would come, & you did:
bright dust
of a hundred worlds
on your feet & the scent
of nameless Calypsos like victors' laurels
immortal in your hair.

My eyes still kept that morning,
their history
brief & blue & quiet.

Yours echoed with an epic blindness
too large to hold one heart.

Tonight I will swallow half my fare
& answer the asphodel glance of one
whose face is lit
with the flames of cities,
whose arms are warmer than yours.

The Darkness Whispers
(Flagstaff, AZ, 1930)
Ann K. Schwader

Again tonight, the search for Planet X
goes on, though Lowell's gone these fourteen years,
& Mars Hill sure gets lonesome in the dead
of January. Tombaugh aims the 'scope
toward Gemini's black interstices, hoping
for two good plates in three, some hint of motion
beyond bleak Neptune lurking at the rim.

Beyond the rim of human comprehension,
the darkness whispers ... & strange aether wakens
to speed the journeying of Those Outside.

Almost a month slips by before those plates
claim his attention. Sifting, shifting stars
& asteroids like sand grains in his eyes,
he stares into the blink comparator
until a single pinprick in the background
reveals/conceals/reveals its affirmation
of everything that Lowell died believing.

Of everything belief can teach of demons
when outer darkness whispers, so men's dreams
reveal the lineaments of Those Outside.

The news of Planet X—soon Pluto—breaks
on Lowell's birthday, though his mausoleum
sleeps mute as ever in the stubborn snows
of spring at altitude. Tombaugh delivers
the word himself—then lingers, puzzling
at footprints sunk bear-deep, but pincer-clawed
like some crustacean foreign to this earth.

Like some tongue foreign to our waking minds,
a darkness whispers: Yuggoth, new-found Yuggoth,
the outpost & the gate of Those Outside.

> "—and I wish, for reasons I shall soon make clear, that the new planet beyond Neptune had not been discovered."
> – *H.P. Lovecraft*, "The Whisperer In Darkness" (1930)

Sightings
Marge Simon

Fritz Leiber
San Francisco 1989
A young writer at your door,
you made no excuses for
the empty bottles, the debris
of loneliness and bygone times,
for you saw she was at ease,
and you were so very pleased
to have her company.

Algis Budrys
Nashville 1991
An elevator hauled
by golden chains, too full
of fans, no space for honored guests.
Though your tried, you had no clout,
the buzzer stressed,
you were refused,
a fuzz-brained novice
pushed you out.

Hal Clement
New Orleans 1995
Your autographs went fast,
'til there was only one in line,
a book by Sturgeon in her hands.
"This isn't yours, but would you mind?"
You smiled at her, said,
"Sure, I knew Ted!" and signed it,
"Harry Stubbs".

Red Magic
Robin Spriggs

This one here, my love. This one here by me. This one here on the highest bough, agleam in the morning light. I've written your name at its core with the two-pronged fork of my tongue and therein spelled your future Self with half a score of seeds. Is it not beautiful to look upon? Red as the fire in the eastern sky, red as the blood of your monthly flow. Does your mouth not water at the sight of it? Does your belly not ache for its flesh? Be not afraid, my love; the jealous god who forbids such fruit has not yet been dreamt into being, nor will he be till the children you bear by the power of the gift itself have deigned to do the dreaming. So come, my love. Come closer. Come closer and dare to climb. Your limbs, my brown-eyed love—my hirsute, brown-eyed love—are every bit as strong as those that beckon from above. Seize the lower most. Seize it now and climb. Climb as you were born

to climb. Climb as only you can. Climb and climb and climb. Now reach, my
love. Reach. Reach beyond your reach. Now reach a little higher ... higher ...
higher ... yes!

In the Earth in Those Days
Sonya Taaffe

> A belief prevails that seals are the embodied spirits of human beings who perished in "the flood,"
> compelled to exist in this form . . .
> — Mrs. S.C. Hall, "The Seal-Wife: An Irish Legend" (1843)

The flood-tide washed them all away,
the children of men and angels of the deep.

The pearl fisher dived into red and reedy seas
and a wing of black nacre and rayskin unfolded

like a prayer across his lips, his wife
dreaming one step further in the saltpan tide

found her fingers enwebbed with eelgrass,
a questioning in the comber's sandy eye:

who is like the god who mantles in conch
and staghorn coral, crowned like a lionfish,

rippling all one name beneath his shifting skin?
The sky shattered them down. Before the dove

winged over drowned mountains, the raven picked

at the floating mat of flesh—their mouths
stopped with fresh water among the salt-smothered,

lightning-stricken, their lungs with air half rain.

And from pearls, their eyes open again
on the breast and crash of colder tides

grey as their sleekness, flashing as the herring shoals
they curve after, all the silk of the sea

to be laid aside like a ransom when their voices raise
a song of triumph, silver as driftwood

from the shore where tide-lines cross:
in the west, the sun

breaks on the water like an old ark's hull.

Anakatabasis
Sonya Taaffe

At least among the dead
I was of a kind, no more
adjudged than a breath let go,
the loosened earth subsiding
under a rainy slouch of stone.
Here sun-demented, railed
by time, the living
tear clamorous as echoes,
their faces memorial wax
overstamped, a cloud of bats
clinging like smoke to the day:
a cup replaced on its shelf,
but I cannot be unspilled.
Hades is where I open my eyes,
the white river flashing
in empty windowpanes,
a coin in each mouthful
to close my throat,
the birdless mist hangs
over the garden's weeds.
Up from the asphalt, the asphodel
gleams like the bones
my fingers were, holding the turn
before one last look
leads the way back down.

By the Dog
Sonya Taaffe

Long before you ever dream of dying,
a stranger will couch in your shadow at night,
slender as the ka that slips through painted doorways,
blacker than silt-tide, a featherweight click of claws,
turning from linen the basalt faces of kings.
This is his incantation: that he preserve you
as tenderly as his resin-skinned charges,
mindful of your breath as of a feather's
lilt and fall, that he pace your footsteps
more closely than any hunter of the sands,
sentinel of the westerly, revivifying eye.
And that he come when you call
in nightmare or delight, a lean flank
warm against yours, a sleek head urging
into the palm of your hand, papyrus-fanned
with bird-tracks and moon-faces

he will not foretell for you; he walks here
not as your end, but as your present,
an amulet I place around your neck,
an earring, an armlet, the seal on a door.
He stands on both sides. He will not let you pass.

Domovoi, I Came Back!
Sonya Taaffe

I left the night, the jazz, the paper circus
with its sawdust of madly loved lines, its ringleader
that boy who wore his suicide like a rose
stuck in his lapel, winking from the bottom of every glass.
We were so cold together, eating fire,
waiting for the world's wrists to run with ink.
Domovoi, all my poems are fatherless.
The mouth he kissed was a drowned infanticide's.

What do you write with in a stranger's bed?
I know these empty sheets, this backward-falling light,
this stove where my shaking fingers slowly warm.
And the poet who translates these words
to a city where the streetlights pulse with gin
instead of vodka, instead of brandy, wine,
will mistake you, domovoi, for a metaphor,
will mistake me for someone who could stay.

Genetic Memory Comes to Me
Nancy Ellis Taylor

It rained. In L.A.
Not rain, really.
No. A haze of
drizzle misting.
And
I went out
without
an umbrella.

Woods and fields
came to me in
moist visions under
the rumbled gray of clouds.

My people. I breathed
wet air. My people
would just throw

their tartans over
their heads and
run through,
slog through,
stroll through
the water-heavy
heathered hills.

And I stepped out.
A woman in front
of the Ralphs grocery
shook her umbrella
and said, "You go
first." I had no
time to explain
why I let the rain
glisten on my head,
curling my hair,
turning it a bit red
in streetlights;
turning it a bit
wild and free.

Yuletide
Richard L. Tierney

The dark beyond my window presses in.
I feel its chill as Yuletide rites begin
To be performed on forested black hills.
Outside, the howling of a wind that chills
The land conveys weird chantings to my ears.
Those croaking tones evoke my darkest fears.
Black gods are stirring in the midnight gloom
As white-robed Druids chant their runes of doom;
Ithaqua smites the land with icy cold
While hilltop bonfires hail the gods of old.
The winds subside, but now I feel a chill
As if converging forces of vast ill
Are gathering upon the fire-crowned heights
To glut on feasts of souls their appetites.
Upon this night of snow and fire and ice
Cold steel is readied for the sacrifice,
And now within my hermitage I hear,
As bright steel plunges down, a wail of fear
And cringe behind my walls, for well I know
A soul has fed the prowling Wendigo.
God grant my walls may fend the Things that prowl
This Yuletide night when death-winds shriek and howl!

A Holiday in Necropolis
Brian Trent

Grandma asks if we want gingerbread again,
third time in a row, disc stutter.
"I've got gingerbread and biscotti!"
Her wrinkled face is a great smile
framed by grey hair like tundra grass.

Aunts and uncles glance over,
fears of senility in their puzzled eyes
as I rush to Grandma, steer her into the kitchen.
"I've got gingerbread and biscotti!"
The Carpenters play in the holiday silence.

Grandma looks at me, face set in a warm rictus.
"I've got gingerbread and biscotti!"
In a shadow world close at hand,
a mote of dust interrupts the invisible symphony.
I jack out and hit PAUSE.

Winter etching hieroglyphs on my den windows,
pipes long busted, space heater chugging in the corner.
My hands stabbing the keyboard,
my hands cleaning the disc.
Too cold here.

Jack in, holiday warmth
The Carpenters and egg nog
my brother's face inches from mine.
Steps back, he shakes his head.
"When did she die?"

Words gel in my mouth,
my brother never misses a beat.
"A year ago," I say quickly.
The family cabin smells of razed pine.
Grandma emerges from the pantry, all smiles.

My brother's hard eyes. "Do Mom and Dad know?"
My head nods, a leaden ball on a stick.
Grandma is promoting cookies again, disc stutter.
Someone suggests we call a doctor.
Someone suggests we call a doctor.
Someone suggests we call a doctor.

My brother looks at me.
"How many of us are dead?"

Images in the Dark
Patrice M. Wilson

I. Death Plague

The universe snapped shut
the night a skeleton walked
among soft women
who should have been singing
lullabies to a maiden asleep
on a marble divan,

the skeleton's thin wife dressed
with the air of lonely penthouse
dwellers who would wear red and
wait for excitement like tonight—

but the skeleton wanted the virgin
this time, canceling the cosmos
for spite,
soft women lifting their arms up
to the sky for help.

II. Life from Death

A dragon-drawn chariot rescues Medea;
later, Wotan's daughters ride
through clouds' smoldering fury,
huge furrowed eyebrows over
bare rough-edged mountains,
valleys abandoned by light
in the view of a bloodshot eye
blinking with lightning,
windy with thunderbolts
while a pregnant woman sleeps
in a cave.

III. Innocence and Evil

After the attack by demons,
a thousand saints processed,
their line of candles
bobbing up and down in twilight,
their thin lives glowing almost fleshless
as churches filled with their tragedy.

Not out of this will come the day
when small children play
with deadly serpents; the parents,
wise, not moving, watch the snakes
eventually go their own way.

IV. The Beginning, Again

Certain pine trees in the snow were illumined;
no one knew where the light came from,
a puzzle of black rocks cracked open
summoning primal shining dreams,
edges that had once touched
and come, fast, together.

Imagined World
Stephen M. Wilson
(For John Garrison)

Awake on the planet of dreams,
you drift through empty streets
to find him.

Once beside you,
now only isolated depression fills your head.
There he stands, sheer, shadowy
"the phantasm who left you behind"
diffusing white moons.

You float nearer,
through a worm tunnel of spacetime.
Love's sails billow and he's sent away again"?
your senses, impressions, memories ache.

Return to sleep.
The world he whispered
is no longer yours.

I, Cannibal ...
Stephen M. Wilson

... will
sniff you out
in the jungle of
N I G H T
 cuff you with
                         blue
tongue nostrils
chew toes
      onebyonebyone
lap moisture from
crevices/arches/pits/sockets—scarlet
         all those hairy acrid spaces
suck marrow
from all   g
bone   r
weight each   e
pungent   y
morsel with
                    hands
                              lips
                  teeth

nipplesnosecockthumbsballsack

beyond
       L O V E
beyond
       L U S T
a hunger
insatiable

I, Cannibal
will
devour
you

The Conjuror
Stephen M. Wilson
(for Linda D. Addison)

An inert decision
the tundra is endlessly white.
Ever needy I seep through
the mindless fissures of

all motion lying beneath
cold bergs, alone with my wand.
Some thing is laughing
in the shadows of ice,
not leaving me be,
slowing my inertia, creating
nightmares. I cry at
the gooseflesh she whispers
upon my soul.
Ghosts swim 'cross my path,
engulfing me; preterit
abysms of time
steal my magic;
man-eating shadows
devour me: I lament
for the father.

The Gospel of the Rope
Jane Yolen

1:
The God of Ropes is strong-minded,
He hardly ever fails.
But should you wrongly tie your knot
He will kill you,
Spilling you carelessly over an edge.

2:
The God of Ropes is crafty,
He can disguise himself as a granny,
An old crone of cordage,
The two knots looking in the same direction,
As you slip from his grasp.

3:
The God of Ropes is just,
He executes judgment on rich and poor,
The noose of his understanding
Slipped tight around the neck,
A snare for the unruly.

4:
The God of Ropes is clinical,
His tiny knots knit the skin,
Bind the bones.
The surgeon is his acolyte
With the ligatures of healing.

5:
The God of Ropes is a lover,
Tying the knot around the heart,
Twining, twinning, wedding one
Into two, into time, into marriage
Let no one put them asunder but the slip.

Long Poems First Published in 2011

Tertiary
Mary Alexandra Agner

Today I took off my breasts
for the first time, the only time,
alone in a hospital room
too embarrassed to look
at the directions the nurse had left.
No more woman, never mother,
no mere anything, anomaly.
Outside this building: crowds
and signs and jeers and hate.
Soon some slang to rob me—
of what? My sexuality
is not defined by lumps of fat.
Know me well enough to know
and I will make you moan with me.
I have made form fit function.

Formless, what can my function be?
I stepped across the line
dividing me from every living thing
when I divided self in three.
Even the aliens, in UFOs, make babies.
As though I'm outside time,
no laugh track, no loop back
for my DNA, my balance gone
as I lean forward for my shirt:
I feel the holes.
Swallow, swallow nausea, pride,
the tannin memory this was my choice.
Empty clinic, clock tick,
time enough for all the thousand
mistakes through which I make me me.

Mistakes never unmade me.
Even in regret, pushed through,
breasts first (since ten),
now nothing first, my knees perhaps
my nose, no longer top-heavy, tipped.
A shirt has never lain so flat.
Fear keeps it still.
More than twenty years of eyes
on chest—never one way to stop them
staring—should have pinned pinstripe
and lace in place, immovable.

Just craters now, echo by echo
changing my responsibilities:
self over generations, selfishness
that generates. A contradiction.

I generate so many contradictions:
stark naked even clothed,
armor of skin too sensitive to touch.
New body, same old me,
but now displayed for everyone
to see what I have always been:
alone, an end. Unreal.
Space is the risk of flesh
colliding, crowd recoiling,
giving hate so many names:
soulless, slut, witch, bitch,
insisting on my sex the less it shows.
Their voices shove and pull,
word-war un-verbing woman,
conjugating human into change.

Still human? Have I changed
so much cars honk and people slink away?
I work, I walk,
same route, same old routine,
now lonelier. Inside out
my lover doesn't recognize me,
leaves no note, nothing of note
except my broken heart—
accept my broken heart?—
too near the surface. Circus freak
in an everyday big top, big-top-less:
titillate the men,
comfort the women by comparison.
No role model for tertiary.
Thesis. Antithesis. Epiphany.

This is. This isn't my epiphany,
that takes another 14 lines—
or lives—at least. I wish.
This is no fairy tale
of tinted glass and Russian dolls
although my dream came true.
I made myself a refuge and example.
Every un-mother in a mother's body
hears this call. Tradition
puts its nails to chalkboard.
Out-sing the screech:

my body is my body is my body,
when I was born, first bled
and bled again, even the day
I took off my breasts.

Star Reservation
Tara Barnett

Grandfather gave me a star for my fifth birthday
when I was still young and convinced I could own
something so grand so completely.
I kept evidence of my proprietary rights
protected behind glass above my bed
and prayed each night to the light in the sky
marked with my name.

I imagined some ancient book with each star listed:
a record of ages, mine on the thousandth page.
Grandfather warned me, cynical and old.
He laughed when I told him
that I would someday visit that star. He said,
"Do not believe of what is given,
that it cannot be taken away.
A man does not truly give a star,
or a planet,
or the waters,
or the heavens."
Such he told me, and now I know it to be true.

I kept my star all these years
sometimes on a wall, sometimes in a box.
As a young woman, when I lost hope and certainty,
I looked at it with sadness
remembering how happy I had once been.
Indulged with a scam, I felt so powerful:
a celestial body at the center of the universe.
My star, my world, my grandfather, my life.
I have none of it now. How could I?

Grandfather told me how once our people
were given land with papers like these.
Papers, he told me, they mean nothing:
a man does not give what he may someday need.
Now the magic is gone from this old world, taken away
with the fish,
the trees,
the streams,

and the sky.
Taken away by those in need:
no paper behind thin glass would stop them.

My hands are wrinkled now and shake
clutching my rights to this battered old star.
How could they know that a little girl's dream
could someday be real and visited and wasted?
It has been used, raped, sucked dry of energy
but I still love it because it is mine.
So easily it was given when it had no value.
So easily it was taken when it had worth.
This shuttle will carry me on to my star,
the one thing I own, that I know that I own.

Let them laugh. I have nothing to lose.
I will not give away my Grandfather's gift.
I will not give away
what I know to be mine.

Occidental
F.J. Bergmann

Later, the name of the town
escaped us. At dawn it became clear
that our hotel room faced east.
We ordered stimulating beverages
and sticky breads, with a bowl
of ashes for dipping. Overnight
the streets had been painted
silver again, and our footsteps
made the tangerine-and peach-
hued stucco façades ripple
with echoes, superimposed
on a murmur of voices from
what proved to be a marketplace.

The booths, in a shadowed square
of sycamores, were nothing more
than gaudily striped tents, each
fronted with a table and a burning
brazier. Vendors extolled the spectral
purity of their flames, but the crowds
that flowed past or eddied before
the displays were sober and silent.
We saw no one finer than ourselves,
although the regional costumes

had a certain tawdry splendor,
with their wildly clashing plaids,
patterns, and passementerie.

Children used a fragmentary sign
language to plead successfully
for coins and purchase cones
of paper, quickly dipped in fire,
torches to wave or twirl, scattering
confetti of sapphire, emerald,
and ruby coruscations. Successive
celebrants added to the swarm
of multicolored particles dancing
on trees, skirts, skin. Even though
no one spoke, they smiled when
glowing sparks rose and scattered
on the smoke-scented breeze.

We envied the rainbow of leaping
fires, but felt that there might be
difficulties with transport or customs.
Then we came to a sleeping merchant
whose tent was dull gray. His flame
appeared to have gone out, until
we entered his pavilion, intending
to ask directions to a museum or park.
We looked out through the invisible
shimmer of heat and saw colors leach
from fruit-hued walls and bright faces,
from the leaves and mottled bark
of sycamores, from the cloudless sky.

Seen through the wavering lens
of that dull, deadening blaze,
citizens now wore unrelieved
mourning, complete with black
gloves and masks. The proprietor
did not awaken, so we furtively
made our own paper twists
and held them over the coals
where a nothingness swam
in the warm air. We departed,
a combustion of abstention
or absence held at the end of
each wand like a false memory.

The Pantheon
Robert Borski

Neither Olympus nor Asgard is home,
but a silence devised by Dmitri Mendeleev,
whose pantheon—or at least those elements
named after or inspired by classical sources—
include not only such major divinities
as Mercury, Uranus, Neptune, and Pluto,
but also a few lesser gods (Helios, Selene,
Tellus, Ceres), titans (Pallas, Prometheus)
and even scoundrels (drooling Tantalus,
weeping Niobe), as well as northern cousins
Thor and Vanadis.

Such is as it should be. For what better way
than god-colored molecules to define
the very building blocks of the universe, the raw
intrinsic stuff forged in the Big Bang
supernovae, or spun off and spat out
through radioactive decay?

If less connotative of wonder and Homeric joy,
place names and scientists constitute
another level of the pantheon. Again, this seems
apposite. How, after all, do we not name elements
after Einstein, Bohr, Rutherford, the Curies—
true intellectual demigods; or not honor
the alchemical source nodes of important
discoveries that fill in various gaps of Mendeleev's
Emerald Table?

Where the scheme falters, however, is modernity.
Delusionally, it's here, instead of reverence and humility,
we ourselves assume the mantles of gods, attempting
to introduce our own brand to the universe.
Hence the elements not found in Nature, but
artificed in laboratories, the post-100 series
of Frankensteinian endeavor created in cyclotrons,
then discussed with great fervor and heat
in the scientific eddas of our time, the dead sea
scrolls of publication and peer review.

The rationale for this hardly matters. Because
by no exchange of logic are we divine entities.

But if indeed we must have them, I would like
to suggest an alternate scheme: that when it

comes to christening our new technological offspring,
we hearken back to something a little more euphoric
than the current IUPAC practice of pre-assigning
names that feel dead in your mouth, leaving
absolutely no taste of wonder, allusion, or poetry.
Otherwise, we will merely be repeating what
the ancient Romans (if themselves on their own path
to doom) did with their children, ascribing, depending
upon their rank of entry into the world, equivalently
mathematical baptisms: daughter Prima,
son Secundus, twins Tertia and Quarta.

Therefore, though it flies in the face of immortality
(the small intense lives of the transfermiums
often take place in milliseconds), I know I would
much rather read about the discovery of Jovium
or Cytherium than Unununium or Ununquadium,
which, truth to tell, sound more like the electron
levels of an onion, or part of some hypothetical
Babelonium series. If man-made synthetics Uux,
Uuy, Uuz, have to be forged, can't we, by dint
of precedence and grace, extol, even if on only
a similarly temporary basis, something like Odinium
or Herculenum? If we do indeed make it beyond
the brink and are forgiven our hubris, could we
not at least have bright, impossibly brief, flares of,
say, Stygium or Gotterdammerum to light the way?

Bubba
Robert Borski

Despite the compassion he bore
for them, some
things were out of the question.

Surgical repair, for example. Even
with a high powered
microscope and an assortment of

tiny instruments, one could no more
put a patch on a damaged
wing or red jewel of an eye than one

could treat gossamer or ghost-flesh.
Meanwhile, at work,
he sabotaged the containers of

chemical sprays, eradicated all
vestiges of spiders
and their nasty webs, left doors

and windows ajar, containers of
cafeteria food open,
toilets unflushed. Token efforts,

to be sure; the best he could
otherwise do
was open up his house to them

all year round, provide someplace
warm and nourishing
for them to breed and deposit their

gleaming eggs. One got used to the smell,
to the cloudlets
of black life, to the insane, high-pitched

buzz of their strafing, and when they
landed on him,
crawling about his pale flesh, he took

comfort, as, in the tickling multiplicity
of their legs,
they brailled his love and affection.

(Was it not the Seraphim who bore
six wings? Surely,
there was a hexapodal equivalent.)

Never, ever once, would he swat
at them, even in jest,
and while the accidental havoc

he's caused in his attempts to rid
the world of real vermin
might eventually be discovered,

although the media might puzzle a bit
over his self-applied
nickname (no southern sobriquet,

but a shortened version of the Hebrew
Zebûb), not a single
one of his co-workers, family members,

or neighbors would fail to mention how
quiet he was;
how he liked to keep to himself;

the gentle sort of person who, under
no circumstances,
would ever harm even a fly.

Dark Rains Here and There
Bruce Boston

i

When she was a girl in Myanmar
the dark rains fell
suddenly in great sheets
of water and sound
in the heated afternoons.

Thunder would rattle
the tin roof and the kitchen
would often flood.

When the dark rains fell on Myanmar
she lived in poverty beneath
the tyranny of a state
beyond redemption.

When the dark rains fell on Myanmar
the sky gave up its color.
Shadows would disappear
for there would be one great shadow
covering everything.

ii

When she was a woman in San Francisco
the dark rains would fall slowly
and steadily for days at a time,
turning the pastel houses gray
beneath an even grayer sky.

When the dark rains fell on San Francisco
the tires of passing cars hissed
endlessly on the wet pavements.

When the dark rains fell on San Francisco
she lived with passion and belief
and drug-fueled flights to worlds unfathomed.

iii

When she was a wanderer in space,
the dark rains fell many ways
on many different worlds.

When the dark rains fell
in the labyrinth of canyons
that laced the southern hemisphere
of Epsilon Eridani Nine,
they danced this way and that
in constantly shifting whirlpools of wind.

When the dark rains fell in the light gravity
of Fomalhaut's only habitable moon,
it was in large limpid drops
clinging to the cilia and limbs
of overarching trees.

When the dark rains fell
on many different worlds,
here and there,
she learned to live with love
bright as a rocket's flare
and loss deep as a singularity.

iv

When she was a *señora*
in the high Mexico desert,
in the steady days
of her peace and resolution,
she would stand at the screen door
just before dusk.

She would listen to the insects ticking
against the dusty metal crosshatch
and watch the light
from a low red sun
encroaching on the deep shade of the porch.

When the sky remained cloudless
on the high desert,
when life seemed dry and spare

as the land around her,
she found herself watching
for one more dark rain
she could walk in.

The Haunted Girl
Lisa Bradley

I.

The haunted girl wears white
sometimes gray
       if it's been a long time
       if the rats have been gnawing the hem
       eating the lace
sometimes her dress looks blue
       by moonlight
       tv light
sometimes it flashes silver
       another warning in the night
       reflecting your headlights.

II.

The haunted girl wears a dress
sometimes a taffeta straitjacket
       choking her from throat to calf
sometimes starched calico
       cuffs tight, waistline sharp
       like concertina wire
sometimes her dress is loose and flowing
       the cotton nearly transparent
       the weave wavering before your will
       filmy as the breath flowing from your lips
but not hers.

III.

The haunted girl has no feet.

Men don't look that far down.

IV.

The haunted girl is only sometimes a girl
sometimes she's a young woman

sometimes she's a mother
        although a murdering one.
But the haunted girl is never old.

Then she would be the crone.

V.

The haunted girl has mirror eyes
sometimes opalescent
        if you fear forgetting, being forgotten
        like barren eggshells
        empty seashells
        flashlights in the fog.
Sometimes they're black gloss
        if you fear futility
        absolute as a mine shaft
        blank as a brick wall.
Sometimes they're simply scarlet.

Because you know you have it coming.

VI.

The haunted girl is dirty
The haunted girl is clean
The haunted girl is clean
        until she is dirty
        until you realize
        you're embracing a corpse.

VII.

The haunted girl has no belly
        only a cave beneath her ribs
The haunted girl has a bikini belly
        carved with muscle useless
        but for pin-up poses and celluloid dreams
The haunted girl has a gently swelling belly
        soft and welcoming
        ready to absorb you
        ready to birth
        an array of monsters.

VIII.

The haunted girl has a cunt
a multiplicity of cunts
too many to describe.

IX.

The haunted girl chokes out her truth
The haunted girl tells lies
The haunted girl singsongs or grunts
Just depends on how she died
        did they cut out her tongue?
        did they crush her vocal cords?
        did they slit her throat?
        did they stab her lungs?
Does she have a secret to tell?
        would you even listen?

X.

The haunted girl is always cold
sometimes she grips you
        icy fingers on your sweaty skin
sometimes she slides against you
        a porcelain princess
        caressed but never cherished
sometimes she is a breath of midnight
        the mausoleum whisper kissing your neck.

XI.

The haunted girl is always cold
I know—I have tried to warm her
I've wrapped my coat around her shoulders
I've tied a scarf beneath her chin
I've seated her beside the skittish fire
        given her hot mugs she cannot hold
I've tried to run a warm bath
I've tried to change her clothes
I've torn the white gray blue dirty clean clutching clinging unraveling dress from
her body
I've seen her bruised shoulders
        her hollowed throat
        her sunken chest

>   her breasts—silhouettes of meaning she didn't create
>   flat and vulnerable
>   high and healthy
>   large and soft
>   silhouettes much-revised
>   bitten cut sliced punched injected gouged burned—
> I've seen, at her center,
>   beneath the ravaged breasts
>   above that hydra cunt and ambivalent belly
> ... Nothing

XII.

>   unabridged emptiness
>   a galaxy deserted by stars

This is the haunted girl.

XIII.

That is why she's cold
>   She is the bloodless chalice
That is why she's haunted
>   She is the obsolete signifier
That is why she haunts and hates you
>   She is the negation of so many illusions
>   she echoes

That is why she's everywhere.

Ere One Can Say It Lightens
C.S.E. Cooney
(for Nicole Kornher-Stace)

When he comes to her, her other, her mirror
She is wiping a dish, she is mopping a spill
She is singing a song she forgot she knew
She is pleased and surprised by the sound of her voice
It is morning, she is happy—and that's when he comes

This is where the wall is thin
The veil like gauze, like a winding cloth, a fray of thread
This is where the light dims, the unlit candle coughs
a scarlet flame
The sky whites out, the clock stops, the sponge drops

Her song is hushed and he smiles

"Do you know me?" he asks
"Do I know you!" she roars
"It's been a long while."
"It's been hell and a child!"
"The child is well?"
"He's my beautiful boy. But deficient in iron."
"Ah, iron," he sighs. "And yourself? In good health?"
"I—goddamn it!"
"You're speechless?"
"You wish."
"I have missed you."
"Goddamn you!"

They stand in the kitchen, half-scowling, half-glaring
Keep steady, no sobbing, no sobbing
And he starts to grin, and she laughs out loud
And their faces are fierce, and he moves in to touch her
But she is his mirror, and quicker, and eager
Her fingers are lustrous, leave trails on his skin

Much later, just moments, she pauses, he freezes
They both look away
"You're leaving. Like always."
"I'll come back. Like always."
"I won't wait!"
"You will wait."
"I hate you."
"Don't say that."

He is fluxing to shadow, he is grayed-out and shredding, and
he whispers
"Keep singing. I will find you. Keep singing."
Then nothing.

Then a shudder. And the world on its axis starts and stutters, and the candle-
flame gutters
It is morning, it is blinding, and the air hurts, and her chest
hurts
And she bites 'til there's blood, and she is so close to
screaming . . .
From the bedroom, a keening
The baby's awake.

The Sea King's Second Bride
C.S.E. Cooney

March is blowing wet and snowy when I stumble on the Sea King
He has washed up from the water—all his nakedness like heaven
With his hair so lank and heavy, green and black as
Sodden seaweed, with his harp of kelp and pearl
Cracked to pieces on his knee

"What ails you, my Sea King?" I ask this creature, laughing
I love him—how I love him, immediate and sudden
The way you love a rainstorm, the Milky Way, a leopard
That reckless love of wild things after years pent in a city

"My bride Agneta left me," says the Sea King like the thunder
Like the salt and surf and thunder
"She has left our seven children, and our castle made of coral
She has gone back to her father, to his bright and airy kingdom
Has maybe found a lover—some brawny freckled farmer
She left me for another."

"But tell me, pretty sea-thing," I tease the lonely Sea King
"What motivates this horror? Perhaps—because you beat her?
Or threatened sharks would eat her? Or treated her with seven sons
Got upon her one by one, and not a year between them?
That might just be a reason, if reason's what you're after.
It's a basis to be bitter ..."

(And no wonder! Poor Agneta!)

His Majesty grows maudlin, how he glances
How he glistens! So cunning, yet so awkward
On these sands that bloat and bleach him, in this shape
Akin to man-shape, gills agape and fins aquiver
How the Sea King's skin is silver, like lightning under water!

"Agneta was my daybreak," mourns the Sea King on the seashore
"I never knew a morning 'til the morning that I met her
When I stole her from her father, leaving only dew behind us
I cried to her, "Come under! Come beneath and be my consort!"
She said she feared the drowning, but I covered her in lilies
A crown of purest lilies, white as beeswax, soft as velvet
I combed her hair with sea-shells, and fed her
From my fingers
Her slightest wish I granted with the mightiest of magic
I played this harp of pearl, and it swept away
Her memory.
She didn't mind forgetting.
I thought I made her happy."

The Sea King's eyes are dark and wide, like otters slick with oil spill
I poke his spiny ribcage and the silver fish that dance there
He jumps—perhaps it tickled? At least he can be tickled!

"Cheer up, my doughty Sea King!" I shout in manner bracing
"For I sicken of this city, of its traffic lights and taxes
Of the emails and the faxes, and the work and wage and worry
So, tell you what, my darling: you take me to your kingdom
And I'll romp with all your children, spin them stories by the daylight
Sing them lullabies at nighttime
And when they're sound and sleeping, I will creep
Into your bower, to your bed of bright anemone, where
I'll comb your hair with seashells, pour my palms in perfumed oil
By and by I'll take you deeper than ever Sea King ventured
We will scour off what's rotting, all these thoughts of sweet Agneta
Do you think we have a bargain?"

The Sea King does not answer:
But he shrugs his flashing shoulders
And I take this for a yes.

It wasn't like a marriage:
No broom or blood or bonfire
But he made a few adjustments for my sub-aquatic breathing
Taught his certain way of speaking, like a whale when it's singing
And a kind of seeing clearly through the brine and murk and current

And when I see him clearly, see my Sea King underwater
(He isn't much to look at—until he's underwater)
Then madder do I love him, love his glimmer in the gloaming
Like a tooth or moon or treasure
That you wish might be a knife-blade so to wed it with your flesh

Sure enough his children love me, seven princes crowned in lilies
We are happy in our frolics, and they giggle at my ragging
At my bad jokes and my chitchat, and the way I tease their father
At breakfast we are raucous, and at dinner most uncouth
At supper, always laughing—well, the kids and I are laughing
But the Sea King sits in silence and recalls his wife Agneta

"She heard the church bells ringing—and she left me, never caring
For my soreness or despairing
Forsaking all her children
Forgetting her beloved."

His wet blanket on our banquets
Somewhat dampens the hilarity, somewhat chisels at my charity
And the boys slink off for climates more conducive to their gaiety

And I tell their father gently, with what kindness I can muster
That our memories are fragile, that we cannot help forgetting
And that precious poor Agneta—please recall, my dearest Deep One—
Had been practically lobotomized by all his fell enchantments
So please strive for some compassion!

"Agneta!" cries the Sea King, "Agneta!" and "Agneta!"

And even though I love him, there are times I'd trade his kingdom
(Yes, his castle made of coral, and his princes crowned in lilies)
For a single good harpoon

By late April I am brooding
And by May I'm truly scheming
And in June I hatch a plan half-conceived in idle dreaming:

"Oh, the bells, the church bells ringing!"
I groan unto my Sea King, rending small strategic punctures
In my robes of pearl and seaweed

"The steeple bells that scream matins—the sound of papa weeping!
In waking or in sleeping, every night and noon I hear them
As if I stood just near them! Oh, the bells, the bell—I weaken
At their tintinnabulations!
Won't you let me, dearest Sea King, break to surface and behold them!
An hour, just an hour, but one hour I do beg you!"

Well, the Sea King doesn't like that.
Does not like that.
Not at all.

He is roused to indignation, which in turn ignites to fury
He is bright as any blizzard, he is cold and white and wondrous
And his bare feet stomp a tidal wave that would have swamped Atlantis
(If Atlantis weren't already swamped from when Agneta left him)
And he blusters and he thunders, and he coaxes and he wheedles:

Don't I like his coral castle with its turrets neat as needles?
And its grottos and its bowers and its gardens and its mazes?
Don't I love to love his children, am I not content to stay here
Like the lampreys and the stingrays and the sharks who come to play here?

How he sulks and how he scowls, how he pleads and how he howls!
But--"The bells! The bells!" I mutter, growing slack and wan and fainter
'Til he grants me what I ask for: "Just an hour, mind—ONE HOUR!"
And up he swims me, grimly
And he doesn't see I'm smiling
 My father's at St. Agnes, where he's often found on Sundays
With his choir, and his piano, and the band that plays on Sundays

And I sit with the sopranos, and I join in at the descant
And my father smiles a little, even winks a droll good morning
He is busy with conducting and he's maybe even praying
Thus I stay the hour allotted me, through Eucharist and homily
But—all in all I'd rather be
Fathoms down beneath the sea, with magic and with mystery
My seven heathen darlings
And a very cranky Sea King

When the bells have ceased to ring, I kiss my father swiftly
He tells me that he's missed me
I let him know I'm happy
(even lacking crowns of lilies)
(even sopping wet and smelly)
I say I'm truly happy.
It's all he ever wanted.

When he sees me rushing toward him, arms out-flung and smile kindled
The Sea King looks astonished, quite bewildered and bedazzled
Like he's never seen my likeness

"Your hair is bright as goldfish! Your face is sweet as morning!"

Taking up his silver hand, I vow as how I've missed him
Missed his scales and his spackles and his webbed and clammy skin

"How choking is the incense! How blinding are the candles
After months spent in the darkness of your castle made of coral.
But it's nice to see my father! Let's go visit him this autumn!
We can introduce the children."

The Sea King's rapid smile is a dreadful shock of pleasure
Like a little boy's first mischief, like a damsel's foremost coyness
Like a man who's given manna when he begged for stale bread
He cocks his head and murmurs through the tousles and the tangles:
"I never brought you lilies."

My goblet runneth over, so I scold him, rather sternly:

"There is time enough for trinkets—
Time immortal, time forever, time for starfish in my bathtub
Time for flowers and a foot rub, time for tokens meant
For me alone—and not some ghostly maiden, be she
Ever pure and pious, be she pretty as a lily
For you see, my doughty Sea King, I am from a doting family
And I know that you've been lonely, and I know I'm no Agneta—
But I'm warm and I am willing
I can offer what I offer, but it will not come to begging
Do you want me for you lover? Or pine for one who left you?"

The Sea King pauses, pondering
(I almost punch his face in) then he smiles like a
dolphin, like a green wave clean and leaping, and he solemnly incants:

"Come down with me, come under!
Come beneath and be my consort
I will tell you all my secrets, I will let you take me deeper
Where no Sea King dared to venture, where Agneta never wandered
You will whisper your desires, and together we'll uncover
All the fire in the ocean."

Then I give my awkward Sea King
This small thing that I've been saving
For a moment like this moment when both he and I are ready
First a kiss and then a promise, then a topple and a tumble
It is frantic, it is frenzied, and we finish in a fever
Come unclasped in joyous moisture
And he leads me to the river
Where we hear the children singing.

My Wings Are Still Forming
Oscar L. Crawford

Be careful what you think
of me
because my wings
are still forming.
Although I am suspended
in the marble shell
of my own fear,
It shall not be so always,
so you ought to be careful
what you think of me
because my wings are still forming.

Even in the garden of flowers
clothed in the fragrance
of an outdoor majesty,
surrounded by trees that know,
you ought to be careful
what you think of me
because my wings are still forming.

I cannot yet take flight
for I am a sister suspended
in my place, the place
where no one notices

and no one really cares,
but my time of flight,
It comes
and I will step
beyond this frozen place
to become what God
has meant me to be.
Like a thousand before me
and thousands yet to come
afraid to live, afraid to die,
waiting, waiting for the moment.
You must be careful with me
my wings are still forming
and I will fly.

A few more seasons,
a few more comings
of the new moon
and the dawn shall come,
and you shall look for me,
the one you took for granted,
always there, never speaking,
never sharing, always available
and never loved.

You should have been careful
what you thought of me
because as you wake to wonder
about the stone one
who has so long
decorated the garden,
waste no thought.

My wings are formed
and I have flown.
And you, you are left
where I used to be.

On the Platform
Malcolm Deeley
(For Gene Colan)

In the middle distance,
the tracks seemed to run together
into a single line, until they turned,
bending from sight,
in the direction that she would come.

He stood on the train platform
with afternoon dimming.
A brief lull in the day's snowfall;
lights would soon bathe
the stark, grey space
in yellow radiance,
waiting.

Behind him was a high concrete wall,
and there were roots and vines,
January stark, clinging to the stone.
At winter's close, perhaps,
they would yearn for color,
to thicken,
graced with hints
that would be flowers, in their time.

As he watched the wall,
the tangled lines of life
in hibernation
opened out, and he saw thorns,
ice-covered, on the vines.

He took off his glove, and reached out,
resting a fingertip
on that tracery of life,
of withered pain, and the scent
of phantom petals against stone.

He didn't even feel it prick,
and was surprised to see
a drop of blood left there.
Winter flower,
a rose,
to freeze and grace the wall
until the sun came.

When he'd died,
only one thing
had been cause for sadness.
Leaving love behind, after so many years,
to wait here
until the day that she would join him.

The lights had gone down
while he'd let his thoughts wander.
He saw, then
the headlamp of the approaching train,

as it turned that distant bend,
and came, arrow-straight,
pushing a different sun before it.

Soon she would arrive
at the platform.
He would leave his glove off
so he could take her hand,
here, where winter ends.

Eight Top Vampire Hobbies
James S. Dorr

1. Breaking crosses.
It takes an axe with
an especially long handle,
but once they're in pieces
they make great firewood.
After all, vampires get cold
on winter-fogged nights too
and castles are drafty.

2. Driving tractors
to plow under garlic fields.
Peasants can be taught
to grow other crops instead,
arugula's good,
Belgian endive delicious,
staples like wheat or potatoes
or beans are far more healthy,
and crop rotation enhances the soil.

3. Avoiding churches.
Collecting maps can be a must
when one visits new cities.
One never knows, especially in Europe
where chapels and abbeys crop up
like mushrooms, what may lie in wait
to disturb one's aplomb
just around the next corner.

4. Dental hygiene.
Regular visits,
a program of flossing,
a vampire's teeth are his
prized possession,
and don't forget mouthwashes,

breath mints, too,
for that all-night freshness.
Vampires are sensitive
on this topic.

5. For the ladies, fashion.
Paris is still best
for long silk dresses
as well as boots,
hats with veils,
sheer dark stockings.
Black, as always, is one's
basic color,
while under the bodice
a good steel-boned corset
works wonders deflecting stakes.

6. Flying lessons.
Sans airplane, of course,
it might seem to come naturally
but there are tricks too,
dive-bombing on victims
in lightless alleys,
fluttering at windows
when asking to come in,
along with evasive maneuvers as well
when bat-winging it over prospects with bows
or occasional javelins.

7. Meteorology.
Knowing wind directions and speeds
is an asset when taking the form of mist—
imagine the chagrin if one drifted into
the wrong apartment!
Of equal importance, a vampire does well
learning seasons and dates,
the setting and rising times of the sun.

8. Gourmet delights.
More an avocation perhaps
than a hobby per se,
one should not neglect sucking blood.

Courting Song for Selkies
Amal El-Mohtar and Jessica P. Wick

Girl:
My mother always told me
to pick up after myself. Didn't yours?
Shameful, the sea-scratched skin on the sand;
it will rub against you like a bed full of crumbs,
like a kitten's tongue licking,
like a lash in the eye. I
will keep it for you, wash it clean,
fold it like a new shirt, put it away
where the gulls won't peck at it. Imagine! A gull for a wife!
Would you not rather have me?

Selkie:
Oh, girl. Don't you know
I'll never press against your industrious hand;
you can't scratch me like she does.
You can't scrape my skin into a map
that tells of where I've been.
Listen to me, girl, you're so lovely,
and so young;
the wave of your sun-scorched hair,
your snow-stitched lashes, even,
especially, your gray as sealskin eyes.
But give me back my skin.
It isn't yours. It's mine.

Girl:
Wasn't mine. Isn't yours anymore.
I know the rules, beautiful,
I stitched them on my sleeves
when I was a small girl, when my grandmother said
the sea gave me my eyes. I know
more than you think, I'll scratch
better than any crab-claw fingered sea-cow.
I know
how to knot the wind into my hair
how to nail the tide to a door
how to bottle up a wish, sweep fortune from the shore.
It's only I haven't had to yet. Don't leave,
don't go, not 'till I've had my fill of you, salt boy,
sweet boy. You smell like the round white moon,
like waves and sea-glass,
like the air before dawn.
This skin just smells like fish.

Selkie:
I see you're very wise.
Give me back my skin.
It isn't yours. It's mine.

Girl:
Was yours. Now mine.
Ours, if you'll come a little closer.
Silky, sweetsea, I love you, I want you,
you're nicer than the other boys, your voice
is dawn silver silk water cool on my cheek,
and I want to kiss you, I want
to be a ring 'round your finger, seal-boy, beauty,
I want to pull you in and play you like a flute.
I could love you so hard, so strong,
they'd write songs of us. Come home, selkie,
come home with me. My bed is too dry, my sheets
too bland; they want salting, sweet thing, they do.

Selkie:
And what of my want?
I can't speak; I can't say no.
Not when you've where I'll go in your hands.
I will go to your home.
I will stay in your bed.
I will stray from the mouth of the sea;
I will sing when you ask, and laugh when I want;
I'll wear boots, I'll work with wood, I'll work you.
I will comb your dry hair and palm your sharp hip.
I'll coax the sea out of your bones;
but then I'll coax the sea out of your eyes.
So love me as hard, as strong as you can;
you keep the waves from me and I,
precious-girl, jewel-box, little-gull,
won't stop myself: I won't be able to touch it
except when you weep, so you'll weep
until you can't lick your mouth for the salt.
But I'll take it; I'll kiss you, little bee,
when you smell of laundry,
when you smell of juniper, of moss,
of wine, of wonder, of longing,
of coffee, but beneath it all you'll smell of brine.
Listen, girl. Give me back my skin.
It isn't yours. It's mine.

Girl:
I know the rules, I told you, I know them.
Your skin is mine, but the story's yours.

That's fine as a rainless day, sea-lad,
fine as honey from my grandma's hives.
I don't want your story. I want your hands, your neck
beneath my fingers, your sea-soft hair,
your strange eyes and your slipperiness.
I want your skin. I have it. You'll get it back in time,
when the story wakes like a thunderhead
to split my sky apart. I'll cry,
I'll slick the sand to silk for you,
I'll pour my eyes all out, and you
will never love me like you'll love to leave me,
but I want you all the same.

Selkie:
Please. Give me back my skin.

Girl:
No.

The Winter Tree
Amal El-Mohtar

It is like this.

There is a tree in me; slim as a wrist
it branches, and leaves obscure the bark.
It is dense and rich, a fine home
for robins, finches—colours dart
between my ribs, thread golds and scarlets
around my bones, spill in and out of flight
as I breathe.

I look at you, and it winters.

Bare-boughed, skeletal crookings claw
into my throat, clatter cold,
send frosted silver spindling ache
into the smell of smoke,
the taste of snow. A wind
stiff as your spine
whimpers the buds to tightness,
coaxes sleep without dreams
of other seasons.

And it is beautiful, understand,
it is so beautiful,
a sky empty as broken glass

a sun streaking ice-light in my skin—
it is beautiful as tears are beautiful
in stories: diamantine,
crystal
adamant
with liquid at its heart
and salt.

Sometimes the tree is a wound.
Sometimes it is an etching in my chest
a tidal river shaped in branches,
silted low, flooded high,
inviting in the sea—

sometimes, the tree speaks
without a mouth. Sometimes
it rustles twig-talk at your eyes,
reaching for a green, for a summer
that could have been.

Sometimes, the tree sings,
keens broken lines and lullabies,
murder-ballads, loneliness,
paper-bark and thorns.

It sings,

I will be a tree of salt for you—
of waves and wanting, washing clean—
and grow to the light of the moon you are,
wax and wane through briny roots
that leech the lymph from me.

I will be a tree of salt for you
because for all that I look back, and back,
I am never made a pillar,
and any step I take
will be away from you.

I will be a tree of salt for you,
and this ache I bear
will be the sky.

When the tree is quiet,
I sleep.

Beyond Our Control
Hugh Fox and Eric Greinke

The first thing we saw upon arrival was
the salamander legs and bat-black eyes
that emanated from a face of
distant stellar cold light years
that was strangely familiar
from ancient demon-goddess dreams
where eternal fire flares from onyx eyes
and the body hills and valleys whisper
secret messages from defunct deities
that resurrect in your word/dream-made-flesh
world made fresh, reborn but left
still unreachably distanced from our hungry claws
our dry wooden legs, our feet of hot lead
and the unspeakables that have been destroyed by
our insatiable need for
not merely flesh, but a one-way escape into the world of
cosmic words, to burn like the phoenix
firebird and fire-sun town, extended old-time years of
mysterious departures, new stars and endless music
when our neolithicism neos into a final Lascaux NOW
when our geological geos into a new Magritte THEN

The perfect spruce shaded house on the edge of
sub-rural oblivion, where the loud boys
are out in the thaw-warm basketball driveways
staring at the raw girls and their confused
parents who are trying to decide if it's time to
stage an orderly retreat or verbalize a warning
as they try to megathink the relationship between
greasy abandoned keyboards and feeble mountain peaks.
Ancestral valleys, streams, lagoons, earth that says
nothing but means everything, its seas awash with
memories of ancient comers and goers:
all lost islands beneath green eternity.

New season, new eyes, new whys, months of hibernation
and right back into the tragic comedy that is
the too-soon evaporation of wives, lives, prizes into
a past not so remembered as dreamt.
Trying to fashion a new Now out of the sun-bolts
that flash into the third eye
at the center of all our evolutionary divine
primetime crimes, insatiable caverns and
the Roman-Gringo U.S. empire dissolving into
noxious toxicity, cancer on the body electric.
Trying to slide back into pre-everything but

slipping instead into black holes of memory,
Polish-sausaging and potato-pancaking through
memorial masquerades that mimic lost moments,
that only return in the himalayas of night. We want
only to sleep in the arms of eternal sunshine,
until the moonless moonlight of forever
washes us in the warmth of happy infinity.

Television tarts throw tantrums for our entertainment.
How about leg-smiles and evening cloud beds instead of
blaring banalities and glaring greedheads, 24/7?
Merging into the deer and wild turkey rebirthing the world,
we forget the inane strangeness of man,
move into a gunless, bombless, swordless world with
the holy animals of love, with the haloed trees and sky.
At night we climb dream-hills to the sun plateaux,
we join the spirit that stirs the stars in their migration into
this infinity that we share, going into spaces where we find
new selves in sand and storms, swimming in the growling wind.
Wife night in the yawn-light approaches our beds
in the black robe of love that contains every color.
Eighty-four becomes forty-eight, twenty-four, as we rebirth into
our own babies, tabula rasa, new into each moment.
Tara-star leads us down paths of enlightenment that
work like waves turning back on themselves,
washing us clean of conceptions of
love and hate, to a perfect neutral state.

Sometimes even here we'll see a calm Buddha face
in a crowd of wound-up alarm clocks, and we have to
clear off the blackboards and windows of our spirits
and send them back to the school of rockabye baby.
"*C'est temps,*" our ancient, ancestral voices whisper,
though they chirp like hungry baby birds.
Time to put aside potato famines and guillotines,
mass mental breakdowns and apocalyptic atomic submarines.
Find a forest with a clear path that leads to the hills of
heaven, if you can. Find it in mind or on land.
Let the Lords and Ladies, Kings and Queens play their games,
changing nothing but seeing self-portraits everywhere, they
forget the plow, the prow, the expansion into
the depth of loved eyes, the soaring heights of
history erased by today's irises, poppies, rain, hands, legs
that carry us through the insanity of human conceit
into the why-wherefore-why-not heart of TO BE,
despite the dry, bare ground where no seed
falls, and if it did it would squirm a moment and then
burst into an infinite explosion of rebirth, endlessly
screaming "More, more, more!"

The music of the spheres caresses our ears.
The wind off the lake caresses our faces.
So what gives with all the caressing?
The message is clear, not bullhorn rips nor
bulldog nips, nor Bette Davis lips. But,
night sky skin that whispers
secret sacred songs into our bulls eyes.
The reincarnation of a million years of Celtic, Slavic, Mosaic
Beatific, Platonic essences, blossoming red poppies in our
hands, waiting for the right Incarnation to hand them to.

Floating through the night, the soul returns at daybreak.
We begin the journey through guava-oatmeal, cappuccino,
morning still wet with dream memories,
facing another in one of the hundreds of eat-spots
that line these nostalgic streets, these streets of
falafal and hot dogs, tacos and Bulgarian chicken wraps,
Mongolian barbecue shacks and premature heart attacks.
Loving the old, old ladies with their white hair, skinny legs
that came so far, their eyes reflecting lost desire.
At last having come to terms with Reality, opening up their
minds to realize that every minute counts, they
are incarnations of the Great Mother goddess who dwarfs
even the phallic mountains in her sphere of love.
We begin again and again our-towning it the best we can,
but the play turns to end-game, waiting for Godot,
who still doesn't come as terrace-overlooking-the-river day
old-man, but instead a cosmic femininity, a presence of
flowers and hills and forests, lakes, ponds, wide acres of
holy lifeblood water, shining out to space.
It wraps its cosmic presence
around each floating soul, newborn but old.

C'est temps for hands and eyes, tongues and bodies stretched
from seed to sea, currents flowing through the body electric,
the mind expanding out of cybernetic screens into the warbling,
warping net of omnipotent time, and farewell to
rhino-crocodile fanged-clawed murdering man-woman,
and good-bye to schizophrenic train wrecks and unsympathetic tsunami,
unbreathable downtowns and the Thornton Wilder-less evening news.
Gone the pale pastel rooms festooned with fading family portraits,
antique grandmas paprikaing red-onioned beef into taste-bud ecstasy,
newborn babies bawling their protests against the sudden light.
School, graduation and the next generations come,
and then they're gone, sand scattered on the big beach.

We have been carried along by a flood of songs,
mostly in languages we didn't understand as the audio-visual world
wasn't our reality, but the melodies played around us as

wind-tree bird-song thunders that brought us back to our real selves,
yet forward and away from our selves too, into a long
immersion in the sensual celebrations of
sub-atomic love down ancient genetic pathways.
We move into nightly real-and-dream-land and march along
the long black highway of history, our voices histrionic and
filled with Finnegan brogues and schmoozing with
Quixotes that joust with the vibrant windmills of memory.

The spirits of our ancestors waft around us,
haunt our whys and why-nots, wherefores and where-nexts,
remind us that soul music is in us all,
and the evening disaster-news has nothing to do with
the neutral universe that neither loves nor hates us.
Simply BEING here on the Galilean earth as it
spins irrevocably through illusionary space and time
is enough, even though the celestial warbling stops before
the great silence at the center, where nothing
but memories take off for their v-shaped migrations into
a south beyond the frozen pole of this poor planet.
Never thinking about asteroids, decreasing planet-weight,
nor black holes that suck up whole living galaxies,
we somehow believe that our cattails and ancient ruins are not
illusions, due to circus stanzas beyond our control.

Wreck-Diving the Starship
Robert Frazier

> "Of those who arose from a frozen sleep and fought their way toward the ocean's surface,
> toward the future on this distant world, only the strongest persevered. Our ancestors were
> forged diamond-hard, tested by extreme, chosen by fate, yet prepared only in their hearts.
> We owe them our reverence."
> *Book of the Original Survivors, 2217*

1.
things that cannot happen should not happen
      yet there my daughter swims into the glow of my diving lamps
      I imagine temporal anomalies or some deepwater cold equation

for Mira seems more palpable than the daily quanta of minutes
      since I saw her life swept away so many summers ago
      flung by the currents that often haunt the wreck of *Homeseeker*

but how can this happen ... let me shift back to this morning
      when I awoke in quarters breathing the familiar perfume of fear
      of sea air and exhaust and the sweat of restless salvage divers

2.
sunrise and six of us set a plan for reaching
    the less-plundered decks by reverse-tracing a path
    that the ship's passengers once made to freedom

first I checked my blends then pony tanks then the holomaps
    dive prep is crucial when your jury-rigged space suit
    can balloon suddenly and lift you to glorious embolism

3.
two klicks out two hundred meters down
    off these alien shores colonized by our unwilling ancestors
    every one of us felt the vast presence of the ship

after two plateaus the descent opened up to a rocky shelf
    her main section lay beside a precipice that dropped to nothing
    I imagined an immense beast at rest in its foreign boneyard

the ship had lost its integrity and its raptor-like shape
    obscured by whiptail kelp and a massive school of butterfins
    that poured from a hull breech like crime-scene tape

we swam into an inky dark cut only by our blue visor lights
    started along rope-marked passages we call the Trail of Hearts
    illuminating skeletons embalmed in weedy suits and

spagettied cables and knife-edged bulkheads and docking stations
    sealed forever from space all the realities of a shattered lifeboat
    plus the myths that have crusted about her and clouded reason

4.
one: she is our true mother a holiness calling us back to
    the frosty chambers where she'd suspended us for centuries
    two: she is merely ill-fated and curses all who dive her

three: a theorem I found unsettling but ultimately worthy
    Homeseeker is the embodiment of death transformed
    a malevolence still active still cogitating still in control

nonetheless we'd come here to exorcise such sentiments
    and dive her for her last useable bits of hard- and software
    to rend forever the clockwork of her immense arcology

5.
the trail zig-zagged from the hull breach
>   deep into the central axis and every step of it
>   >   a dizzying plunge punctuated by breaks to reset our ropes

when a hard current slammed into me sending me tumbling
>   I passed rapidly through alternating light and dark
>   and I felt as if the fabric of my being shifted

as if time rewound in the direction ahead
>   the hypnotic possibilities seemed suspect
>   riddled with as many ominous factors as bright ones

another slashing current carried me past flooded atriums
>   then fatally far into the ship into her Mysterious Core
>   the holy grail of ship historians and wreck salvors alike

6.
as I rebooted my lamps the Core stirred with riotous color
>   all the sea plants and small animals
>   so like yet unlike Earth's

never before reached and thusly unknowable unsafe
>   the huge cryocenter seemed domed with real atmosphere
>   I closed my air valve popped my helmet and

took the chance that could restore my chances at surviving
>   I found warm mists and a ceiling like daybreak
>   winking with clusters of organic phosphorescence

and there treading in green shallows was my dearest Mira
>   a memory reborn only she was not the girl I lost not quite
>   but a complex form whose physiology appeared attenuated

whose very phylogeny seemed to have diverged
>   on a track toward a lithe and compact simulacrum
>   arm-like appendages and the gilled head of a woman

I invoked her name knowing I was senseless disoriented
>   then its/her eyes fixed on mine and spoke the single word
>   that could pierce my grief-hardened heart ... *father*

every cell in my chest blackened burned hot
>   I was truly lost yet I'd found the miraculous
>   and perhaps a proof for the existence of angels

Postlude

it's been hours in this incubator or perhaps a day
       a thin microbial caul films my suit and I brush it off
       and reassess my predicament in sharper relief

chalk one up for the theory that *Homeseeker* still hums
       that some trickle charge allows the ship its brain
       and chalk one also for the primacy of the mother ship

however scratch the theory that her luck is bad
       for pure luck has left this all undisturbed for years
       question: was it my almost-Mira or the ship itself

that sent me reeling and shipwrecked me here
       just another lost traveler
       finally seeking home

Rats
Joshua Gage

One was enough to set a home
on end, like an in-law who stays a week
too long and leaves the cheese and bread
half-eaten. We had entire tribes
inside our house and barn, bodies
black and silky inside the sugar,
tiny claw marks in scattered flour,
tails worming in and out
of walls where there was more hole
than wood. The people say I was born
limping, foot twisted wrong way round.
The scars that scramble up my leg
tell a secret of yellow teeth
inside a crib, blood-stained wood
and screams waking my mother too late.
I grew up dragging myself on a crutch,
plodding through dust where others ran.

The song he piped for us was molasses,
not a pretty tune, but rich
and sticky. I could feel it cling
to my skin and yank the hair on my arm
when I tried to pull myself away.
The melody tasted burnt and oily
like tobacco smoke in a windowless room.
I did not want to walk, but the notes

noosed me, jerking my body forward.
I could not keep up with the swarm
of children that followed the piper's music.
They climbed and clambered towards the mountain
crowding onward while I slipped
and scraped myself on the scree. The seam
in the rock face split like a sow overripe
with piglets, scattering bits of gravel
with a thunderous whine. The darkness inside
smelled of summer orchards. The others
tumbled into those delicious shadows
while I swung myself forward
until the rock began to pull
together, closing in on itself
like a shirt being buttoned. I stopped and stared
where the hole had been and now a fold
remained. Then, panting, I dropped and sobbed
great gasping cries that rattled my body.
The people say it was the loss
that broke me, my slow handicap
that held me back and kept me safe
to tell my tale. I let them spin
whatever yarns they wish to wheel,
but I know the mountain's secret. I saw
what the darkness held, the eager
red eyes and hungry yellow teeth.

Homecoming
Lyn C. A. Gardner

Last night, Dad came by. My sister and I
rushed to meet him at the door, to catch him when he stumbled
getting out of his galoshes. "It's wet out there," he said
mildly, and my brother cried, "You're dead—"
And so it was. I didn't have time to be nice.
"Don't talk about that! Don't mention it! Don't say another word!"
They wanted to protest—argue the morality of silence—
but I leaped over them, back at Dad's side
to smooth his wrinkled brow as we had in the hospital,
smoothing back the few strands of gray hair
upon a dome that had been unnaturally hot and tight,
his skin already hardening like plastic,
red as it always got in summer, as he strained to breathe.

This time, I flung back a look of reproach to ward off their worries,
crouched beside him, murmuring it was all right, I was here—
as I had done then. My sister pumped a red bicycle cylinder

to inflate his lungs. "I don't know how long it'll last,"
she muttered to me, her long, thin fingers as gentle and precise
with the incision in Dad's back that the doctors botched,
as if she was feeding her fledglings, fallen from the nest,
their legs crippled beyond repair, yet still they lived
as she cupped them in her hands, taught them to sing,
fed them, and answered every cry that spoke their zest for life.
Dad woke startled, as he sometimes did
from a sound sleep, so deep we had to shake him,
call "Daddy" in his ear, and he'd jerk suddenly,
call "Whazat?" in a muffled, sleepy voice.

Still caught in his chest, his voice sounded hollow
above the air wheezing out his back.
But this was no zombie. This was Dad,
chuckling deep as we helped him sit up in his crimson shirt,
one of his favorites, and it hid nicely any blood
the hospital or our procedure left behind.
"What did I miss?" he asked me quietly,
as my brothers argued about whether to bring their kids,
and my mother, sister, and sister's boyfriend
greeted him with loud and happy cheers
as if this was his birthday party. I glared at them,
but I didn't dare to comment—it would only draw his attention
to what they did. He was sharp. Sitting there,
hands on his knees like at the doctor's office,
he watched their faces, eyes following one to another
as he puzzled it out. I babbled quickly about a dustup
with a publisher, the *Star Trek* movie we'd planned to see
together (had his ghost sat with me?), remembering how
those other times it was my tears, my gushing, "Daddy,
Daddy, I've missed you, I love you so much!"—
that shocked him into dying again.

He always wakes with amnesia of his death—
perhaps the only way that minds can cope—
is it like this for all the dead? They can't remember the end,
or they'd remember what comes after.
So now I prattle like a child, all the inconsequential things
he's missed, our daily lives, anything
except what I most longed to say back then
while he lay in the hospital, my throat tight
with how much I loved and would miss him,
how much his life made mine,
lest the shock of what I said catapult him into death.
How many more times can his body stand
being reinflated like a bald bicycle tire? How long can I bear
not showing him my elation, my grief?

But I couldn't stand seeing him so bewildered,
in mute sorrow at odds with my fierce, unrepentant joy
at seeing him simply live.

Ravens
Theodora Goss

Some men are actually ravens.

Oh, they look like men.
Some of them in suits,
some of them in shirts embroidered
with the names of baseball teams,
some in uniforms, fighting in wars we only see
on television.
But underneath, they are ravens.
Look carefully, and you will find their skins of feathers.

Once, I fell in love with a raven man.
I knew that to keep him I had to take his skin,
his skin of feathers, long and black as night,
like ebony, tarmac, licorice, black holes.
I found it (he had taken it off to play baseball)
and hid it in the attic.

He was mine for seven years.

I had to make promises:
not to hurt ravens, to give our children names
like Sky, and Rain Cloud, and Nest-of-Twigs,
spend one night a week in the bole of an old oak tree
that had been hollowed out by who-knows-what.
I had to eat worms. (Yes, I ate worms.)
You do crazy things for raven men.

In return,
he spent six nights a week in my arms.
His black feathers fell around me.
He gave me three children
(Sky, Rain Cloud, Nest-of-Twigs,
whom we called Twiggy).
And I was happy,
which is more than most people achieve.

You know where this is going.
One day, I threw a stone at a raven.
I was not angry, he was not doing anything in particular.
It is just

that raven men are always lost.
Think of it as destiny,
Think of it as inevitable.

I was not tired of our nights together,
with the moon gleaming on his feathers.
No.
Or maybe he found his skin in the attic?
Maybe I had taken his skin and he found it,
and he picked three feathers from it
and touched each of our children,
and they flew away together?
Maybe that's how I lost them?

I don't even remember.
Loving raven men will make you crazy.
In the mornings I see them hurrying to their offices,
the men in suits. And I see them in bars
shouting for their baseball teams, and I see them
on television in wars that have no names,
and I say, that one is a raven man,
and that one, and that one.

Sometimes I stop one and say,
will you send my raven man back to me?
And my raven children?
Some night, when the moon is gleaming,
the way it used to gleam
on long black feathers falling
around my face?

The Gabriel Hound
Samantha Henderson

On the first night the Moongirl comes to Kir as she and the hound slip over and under the invisible trails between root and ground. Breathless and rounding an oak gnarled with years and smoke-dark under shade and moonlight, dog and girl run together. *She* is there, small and lithe, a supple twist of moonbeam and muscled like the dog, a feral thing like a scrap of white porcelain.

"Come," she calls, lifting a leper-pale hand to the hound, who bares her teeth and backs her haunches against girlflesh. Kir puts chapped fingers against dogflesh and sings beneath her breath:

> Little dog, little dog
> brindle and white,
> the storm's in the cellar
> moon taking flight.

> Stay with me always,
> be never away,
> guard me at midnight,
> I'll keep watch by day.

>> (when the storm broke and Kir and her father
>> walked the
>> borders and the outbuildings, checking the
>> weave of rowan through
>> the latches, the goats were whole and the
>> cattle were unbled, but a
>> whisper of a white pup sat before the barn
>> doors)

On the second night the Whip comes to Kir as she and the hound slip over and under the invisible trails between root and ground. Breathless and rounding an oak gnarled with years and smoke-dark under shade and moonlight, dog and girl run together. *He* is there, lean and cruel and clever, clad in thin ropes that wind his limbs and pinch his flesh into peaks and valleys.

"Come," he commands, his voice a crack of leather, and the hound quivers and lays her trembling chin on the girl's knee. Kir gasps and lifts the dog's ear:

> Little dog, hunter's hound
> hound of my heart,
> stay close beside me
> and never we'll part.
> Shape of a woman
> please you to take,
> I'll tread lonesome byways,
> For my true love's sake.

>> (Kir's father loved the beast not, but fed it its
>> fill, for he knew the
>> hunt would return expecting its hound well-
>> grown and ready for
>> the chase)

On the third night the Lady of Shadows comes to Kir as she and the hound slip over and under the invisible trails between root and ground. Breathless and rounding an oak gnarled with years and smoke-dark under shade and moonlight, dog and girl run together. *She* is there, tall and dark as the heart of smoke, like an armful of sky torn from the night and made into the shape of a woman. In the soft folds of her gown jewels spangle like stars.

"Come," she whispers, and this is the worst, for her voice is woodsmoke and fernseed, and the hound whimpers and thrusts her nose beneath the girl's arm. Kir chokes on salt and stutters:

Little dog, lover dog,
made for the chase,
made for the quarry
and Oberon's race.
You will be master, and
I will be least.
If you can't be human,
I shall be beast.

(she let the little dog into her bed one night,
for it cried beside the
fire, and in the morning it took meat from her
hand and her father
knew, and her sister wept)

The Moongirl bays and the Whip welts blood from Kir's hide and the Lady smiles, in pity if the Hunt could feel pity, and Kir runs with the storm and flinches at rowan and sleeps tangled with the pack. She knows she is ill-made for the life; she doesn't care. She will not last the year. Her father and sister have buried her old straw doll in lieu of her; they know she won't return. Should another pup appear her father will kill it, come what may. He will not lose another daughter.

Until the Light Fades
irving

There was so much blood on the grass,
it drowned out the smell of the lilacs
but, somehow, not the goldenrod.
No vampire would have made such a mess.
Yet not messy enough for a werewolf's play.
Such are the things we count as luck these days.

Tracking the creature beneath the sliver moon;
a moving still-life in flashlights and frightened dogs
that would gladly run the other way
if not for the one old bloodhound
who has been on so many of these hunts,
the ghoulies fear him.

Too bad they don't fear us

Nervous hunters trudge by a cemetery.
Not one of the old ones—too many still
unpacified—but one of the ones from
the early days, when we buried the fallen
in trenches lined up as neatly as possible
in the hurry to be done before nightfall.

But the devil dark where those memories live
is held at bay for a time—the time of hunting
(Rescuing? Can we have a rescue just this one time?)
hunting for hate borne on blood-soaked talons.
At least this one doesn't seem to have wings.

When it happened, Hell shambled to war piecemeal.
First, just a few dark and hungry things appeared,
skulking in the shadows, feeding in the alleyways,
without even the courtesy of heavenly trump
to warn that the end was half past nigh.

How many thermonuclear weapons does it take
to stuff the bogeyman back into his bottle?
Or back into the rafters, the shadows, the cobwebs,
the mausoleums they crawled out of. Too close.
They seemed to be everywhere—More like
a disease or an ideology than a mere enemy.

It can happen even in the best of families

There are hunts and there are hunts
and there are long tiring nights of shuffling
on half-seen paths and crumbling old-world roads
no one has taken since the cities died in fits
and fires and house to house to corner market to
Last Stand Diner skirmishes and all night fights.

Our children don't remember when there was nothing
for humans to fear but each other, back before you
learned to take better care of your weapons than you
ever did of your car, before life was measured
in moments survived and hunting and killing monsters
became the treasured lore that keeps us civilized.

Remember, it isn't revenge if you still have hope

Most nights the hunters go home empty handed.
Other times, there come a sudden scrabbling,
a breathy shout, and a stench of rotten meat and
too fresh blood as, goaded by the unseen dawn,
a ghoul brings the war to life again, or to
something like life, just for a moment.

We used to use bait. The craving to

desecrate an old cross on a little chain,
would drive even the cleverest of the things
out of hiding and into our crosshairs.

But they took the bait too often,
until we prayed they wouldn't anymore.

Then you can hear the dew scattering
from your feet before the sunrise,
that blessed border beyond which
the enemy sleeps and dogs and men
turn toward home for well-earned triage
and a civilized breakfast.

You can tell the difference
between the living and the dead
by the way they eat their meat.

String Stories
Deborah P Kolodji and W. Gregory Stewart

String-rounded wrists
middle digits scooping up
the slack
(!we were told not to teach
the robot to play cats cradle
but we didn't listen) something
like trestles,
   something
         suspended ...

... a bridge across
origami oceans,
hand-carved chainlink
w/tin whistles
(the robot took every variation
down every path
in every direction)
and every
   culture (@)
has its string stories

someone said, the circle
is the trivial knot
and yet
that single simple loop is the
Planck point into
(the robot sought infinite
design in the
   finite
day shift)

a history of simple story
and complex linear _____

Raggedy Arachne/Andy
dolls and webs spun
by artificial appendages
endlessly loop around
strings with "x" marks
(the robot muttered
its calculations
in nanosecond whirls, such
geometric approximations
not precise enough
for its liking, if that is,
it even had a preference)and spots

primordial moons,
crow's footed double-mesh
nets, harbingers
of growing cognizance
we dream of fingerless hands
caught in harpoon lines
long after the death of seas
   and the time of fishing

mercury,
it's always mercury
shutting down livers
and gastrointestinal tracts
(robot fingers spin
of toxins, complex stories
we no longer understand)
a thing of insomnias sure
as sin and syntax
(the factories tease
metallic teat—
an ancestral alchemy
that draws silver, quick,
from cinnabar to *ssst*-thump
into the bucket,
   into the bloodstream,
      into the barn where the horse
         lies dead)

do not teach your sons these games—
   The Mouse in the Corner
   Bridges of Brookshire
   Owl Eyes
   Jacob's Ladder

Commerce
Territory
Time
and do not...
let your robots
learn to smile
slyly
   behind your back
     or theirs.

Do not give them fingers, programming them
   instead to be competent
     with clamp, tentacle and tine.

Thirteen Ways of Looking at a Balrog
Rich Magahiz

I
Among the mountain roots,
The only sound at all
Was the alarm summoning the Balrog.

II
I was triply lost
Like a chamber
In which there were three Balrogs.

III
The Balrog boiled up dwarf-hewn tunnels
It was minutes to showtime.

IV
A flame and burning
Are one.
A flame and burning and a Balrog
Are one.

V
I do not know what works better
Rocks split by hate,
Or rocks split by fear,
The flame-sword of the Balrog
Or his damn whip.

VI
Stones bridge broad chasms
Thanks to the trolls.
The man-shaped Balrog

Leapt over, facing East.
The grey one
Names in the darkness
A secret fire.

VII
Goblins of Khazad-dûm,
Why do you imagine dragon hoards?
Do you not see how the Balrog
Turns his black-gold eyes
Toward the surface?

VIII
I know the Black Speech
And the drums that go Doom;
But I know, obviously,
That the Balrog is crucial
To what I know.

IX
When the Balrog reached First Deep
A trail of smoke
Arched gently.

X
At the sight of the Balrog
With a whip of thongs
Even Durin's wife
Would squeal with excitement.

XI
They made for the Great Gate
Stumbling and shoving.
Once, a fear shook them
In that they mistook
The shadow of an ogre
For a Balrog.

XII
The bridge is smitten.
The Balrog must be plummeting.

XIII
It was getting dark early
And down there
It was always dark.
The Balrog on shift
Did not clock out.

Anything So Utterly Destroyed
Elizabeth McClellan

What would have been my right hand—
delicate fingers discolored a bit,
a ghost of a ring, a seam at the wrist—

belonged to Miss Clark, believed drowned
in Cumberland lakes, her father to never recover.
He buried an empty coffin, sent her infant hair
for a mourning locket: a jet death's head, not dead but asleep carved

(a scrollwork lie) around the skull motif.
It gleams dully, part of an uncatalogued collection
willed to Matterdale Church
years ago and forgotten.

Sarah Clark drowned, true—
and the resurrectionists cheered their good fortune.
A healthy profit—
that right hand, her liver, the still-flexible joints of her knees,
the virgin center between her thighs alone
worth a gold guinea.

Victor took only pieces of the small-framed, the slight—
bits of bird-boned girls compared in life to sparrows.
He would not build a second giant to terrorize the race of men.

I never had Sarah's face—heavy with
Ulswater, fed upon by turtles and swimming things, deemed unfit

for scientific use. Numbered pages, labeled samples,
but no flesh both nibbled and rotten,
however often he scrawled "filth" and "dread"

jaggedly in rigid margins. Lily lost her left hand, both feet,
a graceful neck. Hannah, unlucky girl, will rise someday
to meet her Maker with no head. He chose her
for the port-wine stain that spilled from eye to chin, a flaw

made by nature, harmless to his results.
Pity the syndic's son, growing morbid in his seaside charnel house.
Sea-salt cleanses, but cannot remove the stink
of furtive purchases from men who reek of gin,
churchyard loam and profiteering, flecks of skin
caught carelessly as soap-slivers under nails,

dead girls' names
hawked like penny dreadfuls.

The resurrectionists reach conclusions,
mutter darkly about perversion and nature spurned, and bring
a new corpse every night. Their pockets jingle with wedding rings,
black brooches inlaid with amber, coins that lately adorned
the eyes of classicists suspicious of the life everlasting.

Virgin, high-breasted—he knew a bride's cast, even
this Eve who never met the serpent, Cain-marked before I drew breath.

What would have been my body
jerked under current, Sarah's fingers spasming, rhythmic,
grasping at life again, Lily's lovely neck stiffening, arching.
Hannah's mouth pulled slack as a frog's. I remember he wept.

I remember not one body, but ten or twelve, superimposed.
Phantom limbs, partly revived, dream of phantom wholes.
The souls toss and turn, seeking to occupy the same space
on the slab, while outside the waves clamor for the return

of Matilda's breasts, Letitia's thigh bones, Sarah's knees.
Victor wept at the sound, and fled, always leaving me half-made.
So Adam found me—too tall for the hovel door, squatting and peering
at my naked, dismembered specimen. If he found me disgusting,
unworthy, a grotesquerie, he did not say.
I could not turn my head to read his face.

Lust mingled with despair has its own stink: sweet like
formaldehyde, bitter and sharp as urine. Victor, more Pygmalion
than Prometheus now, shuddered when the sea-breeze
stiffened my nipples,
even as he jotted his observation of this curious effect.

The rondure of my belly, stolen from a deaf-mute
never baptized, was the horizon silhouetting an army of devils yet unborn.
One cannot trust the female of the species to keep compacts made
by the male, to leave civilization at peace, to accept exile in a country

of endless light, a cave of verdant greenery, a bed of leaves
and diet of berries. I would have been happy with an Eden
carved out in another land, too remote to further trouble
Victor's dreams. I think I would have been happy.

The stone beach ran with congealed blood, infused with salt water,
the screams indistinguishable, pack-howls hurled at the moon.

I had no voice to cry out, even before he dashed poor Hannah's head,
ripped from Lily's neck, against a rock until it ceased to breathe.
Sarah's nails clung to algae, found no purchase, sank. The other hand?
Crushed under Victor's boot like a scuttling crab as it scrabbled to flee.

What safety it sought no one can know. The same coins that bought
our body purchased driftwood, lamp oil, and inattention;
the promontory blazed bright, then stank of spoiled pork for weeks.
A child brought its mother a shell the next season,

a curiously polished, smooth thing, plucked from Thorso harbor.
Thus the smallest toe of our left foot gathers dust still,
among a collection of beads and stones, in a china bowl
kept in the curio handed down from great-grandmother.

This is the interchange of kindness, the wages of commerce with monsters:
a shiny bone, blackened meat, nothing left
to rise again.

A poem for no one at all
Jaime Lee Moyer

I.
A heartless sun glitters off
war-shattered towers,
reflecting memory into my eyes
and scattering shards of daylight
like remnants of my discontent;
the only face I let the others see.

A new planting will see us through winter,
the hope of saving kith and kin what
keeps me walking rows fuzzy green,
singing fragile sprouts strong and high
long after others go to seek their rest.

I've no time to bring grief
into the light.

II.
Night is kinder.

Darkness hides how much is broken,
conceals the emptiness in quiet shadows
softens the edges of cloud topped spires,
moonglow letting me pretend there's life
hanging on in places I can't touch,
tenuous and fragile.

The firelight reflects off worn faces
and valiant attempts to smile,
a deeper murk around the fringes
camouflaging friends and lovers

each seeking comfort in another's touch,
searching for courage to face dawn:
a scrap of strength for impossible things.

None of them are you.

III.
I dream about the old times.

Fox roamed shade-dappled woods
and my spirit filled her heart,
misfit girl-child and wicked trickster
ignoring danger until it fell upon us.

And in dreams I can still
imagine her dodging thorn-trees,
breath harsh and rasping,
fleeing from the hunters' hounds
on legs heavy with fatigue,
and I cry out in my sleep
at the pain of teeth tearing fur.

Another rushes to comfort me,
seeking favor with the witch-girl
widowed much too young,
murmurs his kind words and
brushes away tears with gentle hands.

He isn't you
he never will be,
but he's here.

IV.
Darkness hides how much of me is broken
conceals grief and emptiness in shadow
and I can take comfort in another's touch,
find a scrap of courage to face dawn
and watch the sun rise over broken towers.

Night is kinder.

At night I can dream of you.

Rain Face
Jaime Lee Moyer

The old women my father set
to ward my rooms mock my rain face

light their candles and dance around me,
mock me again with sing-song spells
to lure the white-fox to the hunters,
heeding my father's command
to rid his daughter of madness.

Cunning tricksters
hide behind a blind of lies
draw him into a trap
calling with my voice,
ready to pierce his heart and
not caring they sunder mine,
all so my father can satisfy honor
and hang a deceiver's pelt upon a wall.

Onyx-bright eyes watch the house
from the storm-drenched forest edge
tail swishes nervously
ears twitch to catch small sounds,
a wayward guard's footfall
a snapping twig in sodden leaves,
nose lifted to scent the air
searching for what keeps me locked
behind walls of rain washed glass.

His form ripples and
a boy with ash-pale hair
lifts a hand and beckons me come
beckons me to run with him again,
run until my breath is gone,
until I forget home and hearth
proper clothes and suitors,
until my world becomes cool glades
rain on my face and sun-warmed skin,
winter nights wrapped in his arms.

Windows stick in the rain
and I tug and pull at swollen pine
until my fingers bleed,
fight until muscles tremble and
nails driven into the frame
slice my palms.

The old women prance and sing
and summon my father's
archers from the trees,
ten arrows meant for one boy
who doesn't see, doesn't hear,
ten to pierce one heart.

And I pound my fists
on twilight darkened glass
calling down curses on them all.

Howl until I lose my voice with screaming.

The old women my father set
to watch me grieve
mock my rain face,
fingers fanned in air
as mine splay against the window
blocking the lamplight,
their reflections rippling
against wet, dark glass,
stretching into monsters.

The Cemetery
Kurt Newton

Perhaps it is the stillness
and the quiet
that drew your mother here,
the stillness of rows upon rows
of hundred-year-old grave stones,
the quiet of the dead.

On sunny days
she packed you in your stroller,
walked the half mile from home
down the narrow country road
to where the stonewall runs
unbroken but for a small
wrought-iron gate.

She strolled inside
and patrolled the grass-grown lanes
between each row of monuments,
stopping here and there
to read a name or inscription,
sometimes speaking the words out loud
as if the stones had voices.

From where you sat
all you saw were
large stone slabs,
some standing straight and square,
some pointed at the top,

some branching in the middle
to form a cross.

Cold grey
and moldy white,
some were black
and smooth as glass;
in these you saw your face
floating by,
and mother's legs
moving beneath her sun dress.

In addition to the soft
echoes of footsteps
that followed mother's shoes,
there came the squeak of the stroller,
the rattling of its wheels,
and your mother singing lullabies
to pass the time,
but there was more.

Sometimes the face reflected
in the stone was not your own,
and the echoes
were more like whispers
calling out your name;
your mother strolled along
as if she didn't notice,
her shadow growing thinner
with each day that passed.

And as you grew—
the stroller left behind for sneakers,
chasing after mother's shadow
as she played peek-a-boo;
the rows of stones a maze,
the grass-draped crypt a picnic place;
waving to the faces and giggling
as their voices tickled your ears—
this place became
a home away from home.

And when your mother died
one bright sunny day,
her pale thin face still as stone,
her ear pressed to the ground
as if hearing for the first time
the voices you always knew were there,

you sat beside her
singing lullabies,
gently brushing back
her brittle hair
with dirt-stained fingers.

A fresh grave soft as peat
became Mother's final resting place,
but she was only sleeping;
the following day
she chased you through the rows of stone
and giggled like the others,
so happy
her feet barely touched the ground.

And though the sound
of a speeding car
still frightens you,
and mother trembles
when she recalls the awful
screeching violence of that
day things changed forever,
there can only be
good memories from now on
here.

The Five Known Sutras of Mechanical Man
Steven L. Peck

Mechanical Man s.1

Mechanical man hummed
and buzzed and wondered
on cue if there were other
machines in other factories

Perhaps there was an endless
chain of foundries in which
every possible machine churned
through every possible motion

Or perhaps this is all there is
making his task feel bright,
new and unique

The constant thrum of existence filled
his torso as oil surged through

every moving part
He was filled with possibilities
or rather at least one,
that for which he was made

Mechanical Man s.2

Mechanical man found it
odd that he should be found
at this station, in this foundry,
in this now. What if he had never
been bolted and soldered
together? What if his welding
had never occurred?
His cogs and gears whirred
as he tried to work
through the question of
why he was here
now, being who he was.

If he were not who he was now,
would he be someone else,
say, a robot on the tightening bolt
line? If he were, say, put together
differently, but made of the same
bits of scrap, would it be he
looking out through his percept-o-scope?
That made no sense; he was his
wiring, he was these pulleys, gears, and cables
stitched together into
this mechanical man.

He was who he was, because
of the situation in which
he found himself.
Because of this configuration
of mechanical parts,
although how contingent and arbitrary
it suddenly seemed.

He had been thrown together,
thrown into this place,
made out of pieces of metal and
plastic, he had been tossed
into ... what? From what?

At night when powered down,
and only essential systems
were left running he dreamed

of doing different things.
Things unimaginable, for they
were tasks unprogramed, tasks
whose purposes were different from
what he did every day.

But in these dreams he did something
else, something ... strange:
why else would you do
except to do that which you were
made for?
This difference between what
he was, and what he did in dreams,
perplexed and confounded him.

There was no place to hold these
thoughts yet he could not help but
wonder, as he made the same motions
he made every day towards the same
end for which he was made ...
But ...
What if he did otherwise?

Mechanical Man s.3

On Saturday mechanical man slept in.
His wires were rusting and his gears
were worn and slipping; it was a matter
of time before his fashionable smooth stainless
steel succumbed to time and tarnish.
His blinking lights seemed more listless than
usual and he noticed that the languor of his
gadgetry seemed to lurch more choppily.

He rose to the sound of an ominous clicking
in his mid-torso and looked at the
mechanical woman beside him, her stand-by button
blinking a steady green, her well-oiled
machinery humming softly, gears disengaged.

He walked over to a portal and saw a world
full of machines; he was one among many,
but oh my, what efficiency there was in the world!
Its tick-tock exactness produced an involuntary
clack of approval from deep within his workings.

There was little doubt that when his wires snapped,
or the final cog smoothed to the state it would

no longer catch and engage—the mechanism that was
he would slide to a stop and power down permanently.
He would be no more, but today, on this morning,
he ran as machined—this was his moment to function
and even though it must wind inevitably down to
dereliction, he had at least today escaped entropy's
demands, and that was both sufficient and necessary.

Mechanical Man s.4

Some said reclamation
was like powering down
permanently.

Mechanical man considered
the notion in light of the glistening
oil streaming from his damaged
leg, brokering no staunch.

Others claimed that since
subjectivity was so different from
the rotating gears, and levered
pulleys, it was fundamentally
another substance, like a finer
oil, more lightweight and refined,
more clear than the common unctuous
fluid of day-to-day life.

These argued that this oil—
the true self—would be poured into a
great machine in which we would all partake.

Or be raised to a new and finer
individual machine.
Perhaps one
beyond our imagination, with gears
that never wear and cables that retain
their spring and never snap.

As mechanical man watched the oil
drain from his leg and felt his gears
beginning to grind and heat up
he hoped he would just power down.
He was tired of the endless kinetic
whirling and ratcheting of his motor's
endless hum. Being turned off
sounded nice.

Mechanical Man s.5

After a hundred thousand
million years there is
no one who mourns
mechanical man.

His parts have long since
oxidized and slagged:
he is gone.

But, positioned in that time,
in that space,
his great arms and legs
rotate through their
motions. The gears of
his mind whirl, spinning
his wondrous thoughts,
carving a place in some
topology that only hints at
what it is. And there, in that then,
mechanical man is content.

Stargazers
W.C. Roberts

ca. 16,500 B.C.
the night hunter shook him
tossed him to land numb
looking up into the black sky
the swath of stars and shadows
a blanket framing that face
with ivory bared
to the space beyond

106 B.C.
blood dripped from a blade
falling to the churned field
as dusk turned into night
he looked up, wary of the few
still moving around him
numb to their cries, a death rattle
looking up, he wondered if the Gods
woven into the stars looked down
and wondered upon him
as he did they

1053 A.D.
the smell of the burning fortress and flesh
with the cries of the wounded rose
as he stirred in the muck
looking up into the sky
"please take me," he beseeched
in the language of his mother
as his life drained out
from wounds into the soil
not the stars

1918
acrid nitrates rankled the air
gunshots popping near and far
fewer now in the night
or the trench
overrun by Pershing's men
wishing the stars above
could take them home

1986
the desert had taken his water
and drained him after the bomb
destroyed his jeep and killed
the other soldiers
the night, its merciless glittering
comforted him
with a blanket of stars
that he faded into

2056
power was low but worse
the oxygen
how they hated the stars
their last adventure
above, or was it below? the great blue
mocked, contaminated and unsafe
while the stars—enveloping—flickered
with the irony of having no place
to return to.

Dragonskull: Vision of Result
Charles M. Saplak

DAYBREAK OF THE APPOINTED DAY:

>And yet another soldier will beseech The Dragon
>for his vision; a timeward glimpse of truth,
>a precious deep thought chosen for him and him alone.
>Light's long arrows silently fly,
>chip the mountainside free from night's dark,
>yet Sir Michael has been awake for hours,
>beneath his coarse woolen blanket,
>listening to the sounds of the mountains.
>Wet mist caresses the stony 'scape,
>places a chill within the soldier,
>a touch like the hand of death—
>a beckoning tap he has often imagined.

Sir Michael maintains his fast,
>drinks nothing but clear water
>from a skin he has carried up this mountain with him,
>then he does something he has rarely done:
>he unpacks a clean cloth; he bathes.
>The water is so cold his flesh bumps,
>his teeth chatter, his lips tinge with blue.

He must be pure to go before the spirit;
>must be clean to request this boon.

Most supplicants The Dragon deigns never to answer.

He must be found worthy.

Sir Michael is a man of many days, his hair is graying,
>his skin is a map of scars,
>a history book of nameless battles.
>He has spent many nights staring into fires
>remembering all which is lost to him.
>He has awakened to many an impending fight,
>greeted many sunrises as his possible last.
>Has awakened many times exhausted, wounded, lying
>amidst stinking heaps of the newly dead.
>He has awakened caked with blood, his and others.
>He has awakened to find arrows lodged within him.
>He has awakened in the limp arms of those he's killed.

And his spirit suffers to its core.
>Veins of despair and guilt bleed unstopped.

ASCENT:

    His exegete, rugged and ancient hermit,
        appears from the scrubby brush and greets him.
        Sir Michael knows not whether to laugh or cry.
        His guide is a gnome, not more than three feet tall,
        with face more craggy than the mountain's stone face.
        He wears a bearskin cloak and carries a staff of ash.
        He grins, revealing a rank of crooked teeth;
        bright eyes twinkle within deep, dark sockets.

    He says nothing, but gestures up the mountain's path
        with his staff.... Thus, the trek begins.

    Sir Michael climbs with strength, keeps the clambering
        gnome in sight, tries to keep his thoughts upon the
        Most Holy Dragon, Eldritch Wurm, Older than Words,
        Earth, or Time, Igniter of the First Flame.

    Should Sir Michael be found worthy, He-Of-Scale will reward
        him with a vision bright as fire, a beacon for his
        thoughts and his days, a Vision of Result....

    But the knight's thoughts wander
        ascending to the bone cave,
        something occurs to this old soldier:
        this climb is like life, with its turns and scrappling
        rock and jagged hangs, its moments of uncertainty,
        and in the perspective of one who climbs so high,
        petty lands resolve themselves into placid patchwork.

    Sir Michael longs for something new,
        carries a desire as ungraspable
        as the fog in the valleys below.
    Could there be a greater knight? Could he be King?
        Is he the one for whom all soldiers long?
        And his sword, so often the drinker of life,
        the scalpel which removed heads from armies,
        heads from necks, fathers from sons: is this sword
        the needle to stitch back a splintered world?

    As shade claims the landscape, Sir Michael attains the
        summit, and stands before his guide.
        Rugged hermit gestures the soldier to kneel,
        gestures for him to bow his head, points out the
        entrance to the Cave of Skull with crooked finger,
        Steely glint within his eyes, a knowing-pity grin....

NIGHT, AND DREAM:

At first he cannot see it;
        thinks it just a cave in the mountaintop; then
        it is revealed as the sun touches the far mountains.
        Sir Michael sees the arched brow, the time-worn eye
        sockets, the welcoming arch of sword-sharp teeth ....

At the exact moment the sun dips below the horizon
Sir Michael stoops to enter the cave of the skull.
        Once inside he knows that this was indeed A God;
        he feels the surge of magic herein
a dome of thought, a bone lens of dreams,
crux of possibilities, ivory cathedral where all pasts are
 remembered and all futures can be imagined,
channel of time's dark rivers,
home of echoed eyes through which all presents are watched;
strange stars and secret seas, blood red magma mountains,
 crystalline blue castles of ice—
such distant glimpses interest Sir Michael not.

This night it is his own future he wishes to see.

Sir Michael curls down on the soil floor, draws his cloak,
hears the wind howl, sees stars creep past the sutures,
lies awake and questions all, his mind churning ....

And yet at last he sleeps—
receives the far dream, the thought beneath the stars,
the map of his ambition, his endeavor ....

A distant field he sees,
        site of some great battle,
        arrows decorating skeletons like thorns,
        strewn about are broken spears, shattered helms,
        tarnished greaves and hacquetons still tied around
        bleached bones by straps of rotting leather.

And then Sir Michael feels the jolt of recognition:
        one assembly of bleaching bones wears his armor, and
        within that skeleton's loosened grasp is his sword,
        lying abandoned and rusting ....
        This soldier recognizes himself—
blood-stained spear lodged within his ribcage, and
scratching, scrabbling, curled
within his emptied skull, nestled warmly,
a field mouse sleeps, and dreams. ...

Blatta Infernalis
Robin Spriggs

The roaches in *his* house were not like the roaches in your house or your mother's house or, in fact, like any other house in the world. He could not, by his own admission, speak for the roaches that may or may not have existed *outside* of houses (whether his own or any other), for this—as he had humbly confessed on more than one occasion in a former, more active life—was not his area of expertise. But any and all roaches that had ever existed or would ever exist within the confines of any *house* that had ever existed or would ever exist (at least within the realm of *human* experience)—these he could speak for, though the only ones that demanded it (thereby proving his point) were those of his own abode.

Why creatures of such transmundane intelligence had chosen him—with his stutter and lisp and woefully lazy *r*'s—as their primary (perhaps only) mouthpiece, he had never understood, but choose him they certainly had, and who was he to argue?

By day they had so little to say, and remained so well hidden, it was almost as though they had ceased to be, or (perish the thought) had ever been at all. But at night—ah! at night! At night they poured forth from the walls like the black waters of a netherworld sea, filling up not only the abyssal emptiness of his ancient domicile, but also (by virtue of dictation) that of his mind and heart, or at least what passed for such.

Then, without fail, the otherwise dormant man would spring to sudden life, cavorting from chamber to chamber like a djinn-jigged marionette, giving voice to the multitudinous pronouncements that would otherwise have burst him at the seams. And, driven ever upward by the power of words, he would find himself at last on the steep tin roof of the house, from which vantage point he could feel his every utterance passing into the dreams of sleepers the world over, changing the shape of their minds, altering the paths of their souls, modifying the very nature of the universe itself.

But by and by the dawn would break, as the dawn always does, and in that very instant the torrent of words would cease, and the man—suddenly shrunken to a tenth his borrowed size—would descend again into the bowels of the house, to cower in some lightless nook or cranny and await the return of his gods.

Seasons of the Worm
W. Gregory Stewart and David C. Kopaska-Merkel

I do not mark the seasons of the Worm
   its girth: immeasurable
   its length: theoretically finite

   its origin: unknowable
   its ending: unimaginable

I mine its literature; I mind inscriptions made
    in pebbled hide
    I record the legacies of
    divers races, cultures, peoples
    scavenger in shadowed ruins

of far, forgotten civilizations:
    the social primi-form;
    the fossil tongue;
    the early xeno-meme
    blast silhouettes of supernovae

and psychic echo among
    the background noise

        of microwave
        Doppler galaxies
        and scream.

We THINK
    it seeks a history
    of thought, emerging gods, or
    the early twitch
    of reason

We scorn those who worship
    its physicality
    its historical continuity
    even the cultural icons its
    integument explodes/records
Some say the Worm divides the world
    logic dictates the Worm
    itself is the world's rim.

    What's beyond
    Philosophers ask

Given: the Worm seeks perfection yet
    no sense organs adorn its flanks
    we conclude that perfection lies beyond us
    "good enough" our goal

    mediocrity the new excellence

Others have written (on segments
    now long gone) that perfection's
    in us or nowhere

that the Worm's the world's
　　　expression of our achievement

I have myself recorded Worm thoughts
　　　that if the Worm's our rim
　　　and we all there is there's nothing
　　　I have recognized no reply
　　　in two years' Worm-scanning since

discovering its Midgardian gimmickry

　　　—it cavorts, transporting form
　　　from caducous to caduceus—
　　　it is less hypnotic than soporific,
　　　and it flicks no tongue,

having none. It stares eyeless into my soul—

　　　(its midpoint: indeterminate
　　　its length: only theoretically finite
　　　its alpha: something Planck
　　　its ending: will involve the heat death

of a pit-viper brane.)

crossroads
J.E. Stanley

> *"went down to the crossroads*
> *...tried to flag a ride"*
> 　　　--Robert Johnson

i.
lady,
weeping

ii
soul bartered,
guitar enveloped
in blue flame

iii
four directions
none toward home

iv

        R
        O
        A
        D
        S

          N
PAST   NOW   FUTURE
          T

        T
        A
        K
        E
        N

v
a minute fracture
in time,
the man and woman
cross
without meeting

vi
moonlit shadow
on black asphalt
in the black night
one black bird
one word

vii
frozen by indecision,
knowing what he knows,
a wrong turn means
another season in hell

viii
midnight summons
a circle of twelve crows
a lone crow in the center

ix
the single street lamp
beyond the dim circle of light
nothing but the void

x
cacophony of rain
explosions of thunder
lightning scars the concrete

xi
stained pavement,
the tinge of spent powder
the coppery odor of first blood

xii
a cartesian origin
here
all roads begin
all roads end

xiii
what I need
is mercy
but all I ask
is a ride

Autumn Chill
Richard L. Tierney

Howdy, young fellow! What brings you down here
To this old graveyard in the piney woods?
Not many folks come wandering this way.
Lost, you say? Well, I figured you must be.
This family plot of mine's a right far piece
From any town. But, don't you worry none,
Just keep on this dirt road 'bout two miles more
And it'll bring ye to the Aylesbury Pike.
But why not stop and rest a spell, young sir?
The evening's fair and clear, and I don't get
Much chance to chat and hear the outside news
      From folks like you just passing through.
Yes, yes, I know you can't stay long,
      But bear with me a bit.
I'm a mite lonely here since brother Ned,
My only close kin, recently passed away.
Come on, I'd like to show ye 'round this place,
If you can spare some minutes from your trip.
Good! I won't keep ye long. Come, follow me.
The evening's mild and mellow—aye, and look!
There's bright Orion climbing up the sky.
      See how his jeweled sword-belt gleams!

And here comes Sirius, nipping at his heels!
Just hear that night-breeze starting up to whisper—
Listen to how it makes the dry leaves rattle
        Like skeleton spiders!
A sad and spooky time o' day it is,
The sun gone down behind the piney ridge,
The autumn afterglow a-fading out.

But look, here's what I wanted you to see—
This ancient graveyard nestled 'midst the trees.
It's old, young sir, older than this Republic,
And 'most all of my kin lie buried here.
Look how those headstones hump up from the moss
With skulls and crossbones carved upon their faces.
        They're centuries old, some of 'em.
But see that fresh-dug mound and wooden cross?
Poor Ned was buried there a week ago.
Ain't even got a proper headstone yet.
Ned, he was sort of odd and troublesome,
You know, like some of closest kinfolk are,
But I was mighty heartstruck when he up
And died so sudden. . . . But my God! *What's that?*
You seen it too, young fellow, didn't you?
Looked like a possum running fast, you say?
        Well, I allow you may be right.
Just let me catch my breath a bit. 'Twas quite
A shock to see that critter scuttling from
Ned's grave. You're right, it must have been a possum. . . .
Shaking, you say? Well, yes, I guess I am.
Gave me a start, that critter did, and I've
Been brooding some about poor brother Ned.
He'd read these books Great-grandpa'd handed down
Full of strange things most folks don't know about.
Our family goes a long way back, y'know,
And some of them has had the wisdom-gift.
Ned, now, he had it too, I guess, 'cause soon
After he'd studied them old books awhile
The folks he didn't like took sick and died,
Like cousin Henry and old Auntie Liz,
And when he started looking dark at me
I took to sleeping with an ax at hand.
They say a grave can't keep a sorcerer,
But surely if his head's been split in half
He can't—
        My God! That hole above Ned's grave—
It don't look like no possum could have dug it,
For look at how the fresh black dirt is mounded
As if it's been *pushed out!* And now, what's *that*—?

A rustling in the weeds, heading this way—
No possum goes like that with thin white tendrils
Waving above the grass. No. *No!* It's *Ned!*
His brain's done burrowed up beneath the sod,
Dragging its spinal cord like to a tail,
Waving its nerves like sorcery-poisoned stings.
It's coming for me—see it? *It's his brain!*
No, no, young fellow, don't run off like that,
Don't leave me here to meet that thing alone!
Come back!

Red Engines
Catherynne M. Valente

When I kissed her
        she tasted like Mars.
Like red cupolas, gilt-spangled,
etched steel cockerels snapping
at a dry, weedy dawn.
        She tasted like new streets,
        rolled out like silk rugs across meridians,
        like a girl
who might not remember what Earth looked like,
even a little,
even a pine tree,
even a sea.

When I kissed her
        she tasted like gunmetal cities
pricked with soapy, foaming green:
strange-bred grasses clutching at air,
like a polished sheet of polar ice,
and she dancing upon it, a new kind of beast,
feet blue and bare,
heedless, atavistic, her hair an explosion
which, of course, is red,
could never have been anything other
than red.

In her kiss,
she walks naked through Hellas Planitia;
her pilgrim road all on fire, under crystal,
under a golden sizzle of solar wind.
Her teeth on my lips, I watch her buy
this memory from a bazaar,
drink krill from a pink glass vial,
mate with a toad-skinned boy,

and hold against her small breasts
an ultraviolet bubble
wherein she and I are kissing,
forever,
so very like living things.

When I kissed her
        she tasted like two moons tumbling,
gleaming, old bones cast into the sky
to foretell my own obsolescence.
        What place I, in the place where she lives?
What good my French cuffs
in that long desert?
        When I kissed her I knew
she was not like me:
she knew none of the secret
houndstooth shames
that gentlemen know.
Her Galapagos-soul
had flashed past all that,
and she moved like dust on the plain.

A gentleman comes boldly,
        when he comes.
He knocks at a little round door,
all etiquette, bred like a dog
to race after her, oh, to run,
while she speeds ahead in her uncatchable orbit,
spinning on her silver rod
        always,
        always,
so very like a living girl,
        always,
        always,
so very much faster than he.

I cannot go to Mars.
I am extinct there—
customs would never let me pass.
The days of maids yelping in chicken yards,
scared half-to-death of a hymen
are gone.

When I kissed her
        she tasted like change,
like the face of the moon
suddenly showing her dark.
        I did not notice.

Still, yet in the chicken yard,
thinking it mattered,
that it would bother her,
I curdled the milk and ruined the beer,
unspun the wool and frightened the cows,
crowing at my body's breadth—
while she, oil-grimed, skull shaved,
quietly built red engines
to carry herself off.

My hands in her hair,
I looked up in the smoky night,
to a red thing in the sky,
and began to break along the seams,
to fold and arc like a steel cockerel
straining at the sun,
to sear into a thing
that might match her;
not gentle, not bred,
a thing which might taste
of orange domes like bodies rising,
of pilgrim blood both savage
and serene.

Barren: A Chronicle In Futility
Steve Vernon

Day 1

We do not know where we will find it
perhaps somewhere far beyond
where the water feeds the thirsty willow
where the cattail stands rooted in mute vigil
where the scrub pine scratches at the shadow of starlight

it is out there waiting
moss and antler
wing and hoof
shadow and swamp steeps beneath the mist
as sphagnum swallows each booted step

we follow, pretending some measure of direction
raising and stabbing the blades of our paddles
into a river that bleeds into streams
stained with iron ore
and cedar yearnings

we pass our maps from lip to lip
like men in darkness speaking of dead lover's kisses
whispering names that taste of penitent beads
Sooy Place, Drake Kill, Ong Hat
Hog Wallow, Rivers Meet and Mary Ann Furnace

but worse are the ways and stations
that lie nameless and dreaming
just beyond the yellow curled edge of the map
those places we remember as never having seen
until we have passed them by, unnoticed

in the evening Killian puffs wistfully upon his pipe
and tells us we would not believe what his eyes have seen
talking of wood spirits, centipedal gods, fish as large as riverboats
his words feed our fear with a kindle of ill-founded gossip
and sleep embers fitfully through a long dreamless night.

Day 2

Morning caught the fine early mist
like lamp oil cast upon a burning rose
clots of thunder brooded along the horizon
the wind gossiped through the rattling pine needles and scaly trunks
and a viper was found curled in a bedroll with the scout who did not see it

the men packed gear without words
hiding fear in grunts and murmurs
eager to follow the path their feet would make
down towards the imagined safety of the river
moving away from the darkling woods

Jimmy Fetterman whistled "Old Garry Owen" badly off-key
until Michael Stuart, who was born of a wayward Spanish whore
laid ungently between the cannons of a British man-of-war
enquired if Fetterman were trying his damndest to
whistle up some god-be-damned storm

it is out there, Fetterman replied
like it as not, it is out there
waiting in the space that waits between wind and shadow
moss and antler, wing and hoof
tooth and delicate claw

if it is out there, said Stuart, then I pity it
for Commodore Decatur has forged his heart into a cannonball
that shall arc like a promise of revenge and redemption
across the long cloudless sky of memory
to puncture and tear a thin lace-ribbed wingbone

the river current carried us deeper
into the heart of the lonesome piney woods
we had as little to say of our course
as a carefree wag of dandelion dander
dancing in the palm of the wind.

Day 3

We walk through woodland
in slow funereal silence
tree stumps molar upwards like so many grey splintered tombstones
roots prowl and twist through dirt hidden
beneath a shroud of the ever-present brittle pine needles

branches dried in death
splinter and crack beneath our booted step
bones of granite knee and elbow
eager to catch
at unwary feet

the forest smothers sound like an unwanted child
words are forgotten, tongues fall mute
thought gives way to instinct rooted in bone
when the silence takes Lefarge
we do not hear a thing

we find what is left of him draped from branch
to branch like some mad Maypole frolic
blood pipe and the tunnel of gut
ruptured and torn like a musket-tattered mainsail
in the notch of roots the violets slowly crimson.

it is out there, Killian tells us
waiting full of fear and darkness
moss and antler, wing and hoof
he bows his head and prays for a dead man's soul
as a night crow beaks listlessly at the little that is left behind

that evening the peepers creak nocturnal dirges
and the wind blows in a woman's voice
the shadows huddle against tree trunks
in the morning we find the leaves of Killian's bible
torn and tattered, hanging and laughing on every branch we see.

Day 4.

We ginger our steps fearfully through the endless trees
through a flat plain composed of both wilderness and wasteland
beneath a moon that burns by daylight

the scrub pine and tamarack and witch elm
murky swamp oak, pitch and gum

sing, you godless bastards, sing
Decatur urges us
for we are almost there
he hammers his words with the fervour of a fallen blacksmith
forcing hollow-forged courage, he fools no one

it is out there and we know it
moss and antler, wing and hoof
call it kangaroo horse, kingowing, woozlebug
cowbird, flying hoof, devil beast, damned
Mother Leed's runted bastardly whelp

we chew fear like twists of dried horsemeat
walking six feet downward
with every step we take
our breathing wheezing faintly sighs
a crosscut saw chewing slowly into old punky wood

Schultze—that big lonely lumberjack from Michigan
nothing more than a blanket coat on timber-tall legs
a knife, well-honed, and large enough
to decapitate a full-grown bull moose
swings softly beneath a wolf pine from a well-tied knot

that night we sleep fitfully as
Fetterman clubs Stuart in his sleep with a chunk of river stone
the size and heft of a good-sized prayer book
and then picks up his musket, points towards his head,
and finds forgiveness in a sudden swallow of powder, ball and smoke.

Day 5

We awoke to find the boats broken upon the shoreline
the thin pine skin torn from oaken bones
Decatur knelt in the mud and wept dirty tears
Killian stared upwards into a cold empty sky
shifting slowly from one foot to the other

three men drowned themselves
kneeling in chest-deep water
singing a baptistery hymn—washed in the blood
they lean forward, down and gone
the bubbles rising one, one, one

another beats his head open against a leaning stone
one opens his own veins with his teeth

one by one we fall away through poison and flensing knives
slow drops falling upon fallen pine needles
beneath the empty hosanna of a cloudless sky

in the darkness you will find us
moss and antler, wing and hoof
a map sewn into memory as long as spiralled tusk
chronicled in the intricate scrawl-work
of the burrowing bark beetle's hieroglyphic sigil

the ants tunnel restlessly beneath the dead fallen pine needles
Killian feels his fingers touch behind the holes behind his eyes
Decatur walks with his cannonball down to the waiting river
the hoot owls taunt us, the whippoorwill will not sing
something scuttles beneath the pine needles

the needles knit the night away
whisper, chatter, chirp and curl
sewing stitch after patient stitch
cloth, bone, wood and leaf
as the Barrens give birth away

history books tell us that the 1820 expedition
returned to civilization and wrote nothing down
our bones lie scattered in a mulch that moves slowly beneath a blind moon
that none can see or remember and what came back in our place
has no name that should be mentioned aloud.

A More Significant Sun
Phoebe Wilcox

I nestle beneath the covers, hands on your chest,
and pray
that you keep me tethered.

There was a time when I dug my fingers into the mane
of my pony,
ducked my face into its neck
and galloped,   swiftly, recklessly into a
dream,
jarring my teeth, jaws snapping together in the
landing, the barely-made
leap over the silver rag of water
running turbulent between two worlds.
I came to that lovely land,
longingly into dangerous blooms.
Now I want to stay with you where I am safe.

don't I?

Or ... shall I go?
The pony stamps her hoof,
paws the dirt and snorts warm grassy breath.
We could
leave you calling for me from the other side.
I wouldn't hear you,
not with an aria of an angel's song luring me away.

Not with their hands leading me through the ferns,
into the long-awaited
seduction of blood-red bleeding hearts,
where I would stray that sunny day with the sun
slipping its knife in
to open me like a letter sent secretly.
Let me correspond with a universe of pain and
ecstasy there alone,
safe from those   worldly things
that kept coming and coming and coming
over me. An angel
will unburden me   unwind my binding human
clothing.
Dazed from the long journey,
I'd collapse into his white satin robe,
his bird-like wing against my cheek   green
moss,
a million microscopic hands pressing,
all of it draped in gauze light of a deeper, golder,
more significant sun.
How does   such a significant light shined by
such a secondary sun shine?
It is a truer light than the sun I once knew?
Is this angel, this sun, all in sweet disguise? The
sensation of elation, prodigal pleasure, body
arching in a state sublime ...
Where am I, where am I, where is this, where am I?

From tremulous pink corollas and scepter-like
capitula, I dined on nectar,
weak and drunk, rescued and drowning, pulsed into a
psychic kiss,
sugar-light and fathoms-dark.
Where am I, where am I, where is this, where am I?
And the Mystery returns:

You have been set free. You have consummated your
relationship with the night. You are like the satin

lining of the sky
turned on.
You can come.
You can go.
But you cannot coexist, heart-cleaved, in both
places; you must live
in one place or the other. Gallop your little pony
away ...
and you will miss the sweet music, the sweet nectar,
the sweet bloom
of new color, when you go.
You will miss it, yes you will, when you return

to your secondary joys and pains,
your diurnal ordinary,
your simple sunny kitchen
with its simple
everyday sun.

The Rhysling Winners: 1978-2011

Year	Category	Author	Title
1978	Long	Gene Wolfe	"The Computer Iterates the Greater Trumps"
	Short	Duane Ackerson	"The Starman"
	(tie)	Sonya Dorman	"Corruption of Metals"
		Andrew Joron	"Asleep in the Arms of Mother Night"
1979	Long	Michael Bishop	"For the Lady of a Physicist"
	Short	Duane Ackerson	"Fatalities"
	(tie)	Steve Eng	"Storybooks and Treasure Maps"
1980	Long	Andrew Joron	"The Sonic Flowerfall of Primes"
	Short	Robert Frazier	"Encased in the Amber of Eternity"
	(tie)	Peter Payack	"The Migration of Darkness"
1981	Long	Thomas M. Disch	"On Science Fiction"
	Short	Ken Duffin	"Meeting Place"
1982	Long	Ursula K. Le Guin	"The Well of Baln"
	Short	Raymond DiZazzo	"On the Speed of Sight"
1983	Long	Adam Cornford	"Your Time and You: A Neoprole's Dating Guide"
	Short	Alan P. Lightman	"In Computers"
1984	Long	Joe Haldeman	"Saul's Death: Two Sestinas"
	Short	Helen Ehrlich	"Two Sonnets"
1985	Long	Siv Cedering	"A Letter from Caroline Herschel"
	Short	Bruce Boston	"For Spacers Snarled in the Hair of Comets"
1986	Long	Andrew Joron	"Shipwrecked on Destiny Five"
	Short	Susan Palwick	"The Neighbor's Wife"
1987	Long	W. Gregory Stewart	"Daedalus"
	Short	Jonathan V. Post	"Before the Big Bang: News from the Hubble Large Space Telescope"
	(tie)	John Calvin Rezmerski	"A Dream of Heredity"
1988	Long	Lucius Shepard	"White Trains"
	Short	Bruce Boston	"The Nightmare Collector"
	(tie)	Suzette Haden Elgin	"Rocky Road to Hoe"
1989	Long	Bruce Boston	"In the Darkened Hours"
	(tie)	John M. Ford	"Winter Solstice, Camelot Station"
	Short	Robert Frazier	"Salinity"
1990	Long	Patrick McKinnon	"dear spacemen"
	Short	G. Sutton Breiding	"Epitaph for Dreams"

1991	Long	David Memmott	"The Aging Cryonicist in the Arms of His Mistress Contemplates the Survival of the Species While the Phoenix Is Consumed by Fire"
	Short	Joe Haldeman	"Eighteen Years Old, October Eleventh"
1992	Long	W. Gregory Stewart	"the button and what you know"
	Short	David Lunde	"Song of the Martian Cricket"
1993	Long	William J. Daciuk	"To Be from Earth"
	Short	Jane Yolen	"Will"
1994	Long	W. Gregory Stewart and Robert Frazier	"Basement Flats: Redefining the Burgess Shale"
	Short	Bruce Boston	"Spacer's Compass"
	(tie)	Jeff VanderMeer	"Flight Is for Those Who Have Not Yet Crossed Over"
1995	Long	David Lunde	"Pilot, Pilot"
	Short	Dan Raphael	"Skin of Glass"
1996	Long	Margaret B. Simon	"Variants of the Obsolete"
	Short	Bruce Boston	"Future Present: A Lesson in Expectation"
1997	Long	Terry A. Garey	"Spotting UFOs While Canning Tomatoes"
	Short	W. Gregory Stewart	"Day Omega"
1998	Long	Laurel Winter	"why goldfish shouldn't use power tools"
	Short	John Grey	"Explaining Frankenstein to His Mother"
1999	Long	Bruce Boston	"Confessions of a Body Thief"
	Short	Laurel Winter	"egg horror poem"
2000	Long	Geoffrey A. Landis	"Christmas (after we all get time machines)"
	Short	Rebecca Marjesdatter	"Grimoire"
2001	Long	Joe Haldeman	"January Fires"
	Short	Bruce Boston	"My Wife Returns as She Would Have It"
2002	Long	Lawrence Schimel	"How to Make a Human"
	Short	William John Watkins	"We Die as Angels"
2003	Long	Charles Saplak and Mike Allen	"Epochs in Exile: A Fantasy Trilogy"
	(tie)	Sonya Taaffe	"Matlacihuatl's Gift"
	Short	Ruth Berman	"Potherb Gardening"
2004	Long	Theodora Goss	"Octavia Is Lost in the Hall of Masks"
	Short	Roger Dutcher	"Just Distance"

2005	Long	Tim Pratt	"Soul Searching"
	Short	Greg Beatty	"No Ruined Lunar City"
2006	Long	Kendall Evans and David C. Kopaska-Merkel	"The Tin Men"
	Short	Mike Allen	"The Strip Search"
2007	Long	Mike Allen	"The Journey to Kailash"
	Short	Rich Ristow	"The Graven Idol's Godheart"
2008	Long	Catherynne M. Valente	"The Seven Devils of Central California"
	Short	F.J. Bergmann	"Eating Light"
2009	Long	Geoffrey A. Landis	"Search"
	Short	Amal El-Mohtar	"Song for an Ancient City"
2010	Long	Kendall Evans and Samantha Henderson	"In the Astronaut Asylum"
	Short	Ann K. Schwader	"To Theia"

For a complete list of Rhysling winners, runner-ups and nominees, see the Science Fiction Poetry Association archive at http://www.sfpoetry.com/archive.htm.

SFPA Grand Master Award Winners

1999	Bruce Boston
2005	Robert Frazier
2008	Ray Bradbury
2010	Jane Yolen

How to Join the SFPA

OUR MEMBERS receive four issues of *Star*Line: The Journal of the Science Fiction Poetry Association*, filled with poetry, reviews, articles, and more. Members also receive a copy of the annual Rhysling Anthology, filled with the best SF poetry of the previous year, selected by the membership. Each member is allowed to nominate one short poem and one long poem to be printed in this anthology, and then vote for which poems should receive the Rhysling Awards.

Annual Membership Dues
United States/Canada/Mexico: $21
Elsewhere: $25.00

All prices are in U.S. funds. All checks should be made out to the Science Fiction Poetry Association and sent to:

**SFPA Treasurer:
Samantha Henderson
PO Box 4846
Covina, CA 91723**

SFPATreasurer@gmail.com

Or sent by PayPal to SFPANet@aol.com.
Credit card payments are accepted through PayPal. For more information visit:

www.sfpoetry.com

www.ingramcontent.com/pod-product-compliance
Lightning Source LLC
Chambersburg PA
CBHW051807040426
42446CB00007B/561